Learning to Love

GOD

Book One

The *Learning to Love* Series

Small Group Bible Study on Living the Christian Faith

by Richard Peace

NAVPRESS
BRINGING TRUTH TO LIFE
NavPress Publishing Group
P.O. Box 35001, Colorado Springs, Colorado 80935

Pilgrimage Publishing, Hamilton, Massachusetts

This book is based on an earlier book by the author:
Learning to Love: Book One. Learning to Love God,
©1968 published by Zondervan Publishing House
and InterVarsity Press. It has been substantially
revised and expanded from the earlier edition and its
format and focus have been altered.

ISBN 08910-98410

Cover illustration: Bob Fuller Creative

4 5 6 7 8 9 10 11 12 13 14 15 16 17/99 98 97 96 95

To Judith,
of course,
once again

The Learning to Love series:

Book One: Learning to Love God
Book Two: Learning to Love Ourselves
Book Three: Learning to Love Others

The aim of any Bible study ought to be to bring the reader into contact with Scripture in such a way that his or her life will be changed. This is my aim in *LEARNING TO LOVE*. The focus, therefore, is not on learning doctrine but on learning how to live like a Christian. Doctrine is present, of course, but always in relationship to life.

These studies were written originally in the 1960s to serve as follow-up literature in evangelistic missions conducted by African Enterprise, a group which I helped start while a student at Fuller Theological Seminary and with which I served for eight years in Africa. In their original form, they were published by two presses: Zondervan Publishing House and InterVarsity Press. They went through over twenty editions and were translated into Chinese, Spanish, Portuguese, and Korean. Certain parts of the series were translated into Zulu and Sotho.

But the original *LEARNING TO LOVE* has been out of print for many years. However, I kept getting requests for the books since it seems that nothing quite replaced them. The need remained to assist new Christians in beginning their lives as followers of Jesus. So it seemed appropriate to revise and update *LEARNING TO LOVE* as the inaugural volumes for our new publishing house: Pilgrimage Publishing.

When I first conceived of this project, what I had in mind was a modest updating of the original books coupled with translation from individual studies into a small group format. Of course, as I started working on the project it soon became evident that what was demanded was a thorough-going revision. The result is that only a small part of the original material remains. Most of the original topics are still addressed, generally using the same passages from the Bible, however in different ways. In addition, six new Bible studies have been written (expanding the series from fifteen to twenty-one studies). The result is, I hope, a highlyusable series for a new generation of Christians.

The first set of *LEARNING TO LOVE* books was written in South Africa. It is appropriate that the new series was also written in South Africa during my sabbatical from Gordon-Conwell Theological Seminary. I am grateful to the many people who assisted me in completing this new series, both directly and indirectly, especially all the folk on Morningside Farm in Winterton, Natal, South Africa, where I lived while writing. Specifically, I want to thank:

- ◆ Joan Reeve, who opened her farm to my family, giving us a wonderful place to live, and her father Cyril Gemmel, who always had a ready story or comment;
- ◆ all the people who worked on the farm and helped us in one way or another: Musa, Gertrude, Rosie, Mavis, and the rest of the Zulu staff;
- ◆ the young people living and working there: David, Jolyn, and Katelyn Reeve; Bass; Rob Mark; Joel Howe; Jenny and Jonathan Peace; and
- ◆ the unforgettable kids: Daisy and the three musketeers—Sbusiso, Thabani, and Phumleni, as well as the other kids: Sindi, Thokozani, Zanele, and Freedom.

I appreciate the generosity of the Trustees of Gordon-Conwell in giving me the time to write through the sabbatical program. And, of course, my biggest thanks go to my wife Judy, who has supported me through yet another writing project. "Keep it simple. Keep it useful," she kept saying. I hope I did.

Grateful acknowledgment is made to the following publishers for permission to reprint copyright material:

◆ *Spiritual Traditions for the Contemporary Church*, by Robin Maas and Gabriel O'Donnell (Nashville: Abingdon Press, 1990)—contained a quote from *The Book of Concord,* ed. & trans. by Theodore G. Tappert (Philadelphia: Fortress Press, 1959).

◆ *The Letters of John and Jude (The Daily Study Bible)*, by William Barclay (Philadelphia: Westminster Press, 1961).

◆ *Basic Christianity*, by John R.W. Stott (Downers Grove: InterVarsity Press, 1971).

◆ *The Oxford Book of Prayer*, ed. by George Appleton (New York: Oxford University Press, 1985).

BIBLE VERSIONS

◆ The New International Version:
Scripture taken from the *HOLY BIBLE, NEW INTERNATIONAL VERSION*. Copyright © 1973, 1978, 1984 International Bible Society. Used by permission of Zondervan Bible Publishers.

◆ *The Message (The New Testament in Contemporary English)*, ©1993 by Eugene H. Peterson (Colorado Springs: NavPress).

◆ *The Revised Standard Version*, © 1946, 1952, 1971, 1973 by the National Council of Churches of Christ (New York).

◆ *The New Revised Standard Version*, © 1989 by the National Council of Churches of Christ (New York).

◆ *J.B. Phillips: The New Testament in Modern English*, © 1972 (London: Collins).

◆ *The New Jerusalem Bible*, © 1985 (New York: Doubleday).

Richard V. Peace

An Introduction to the Series

Becoming a Christian is an awesome step to take. In deciding to follow Jesus we are turning our backs on many of the attitudes, actions, and ideas that once guided our lives. We are turning toward the way of life shown us by Jesus. We turn to Christ because we discover that the "old way" was the way of death; Jesus offers the way of life.

In coming to Christ, we are often thrown off balance. It is like living in a fog and having a new and powerful light burst through to show us a completely new path to follow. This can be a disconcerting experience. We no longer know what to make of our old lives; we only barely grasp what this new life holds.

This brings us to the point of this series: its aim is to illuminate the new way of Jesus while helping us to reflect on our old life.

We will examine the key ideas of Christ's way: he gives us a new way of viewing the world around us—a way filled with hope and purpose. We will reflect on the new attitudes that characterize the new way, since Christ helps us to form a new affection. This changes how we view others and what we give ourselves to. Finally, we will examine the kind of lifestyle Jesus wants us to have: what we do matters, and (at times) Christ calls us to stand against the stream of culture.

We will do all this together with others—with some people who have been "on the way" for a while, and others who are just starting on the way. The Christian way was never meant to be a solitary path. The church is intended to be the joyous community of pilgrims aiding and supporting one another "on the way."

A word about how this course has been organized. The three books of this series are structured around the Great Commandment given by Jesus: "Love the Lord your God with all your heart and with all your soul and with all your mind and with all your strength.... Love your neighbor as yourself. "

In Book One, we will look at what it means to learn to love God. God is alive and personal, as present as our next breath. Yet God is also spirit. Therefore, having a relationship with God is different from having a relationship with another person. We need to consider how one grows and nurtures a relationship with the living God.

In Book Two, we shift the topic from God to ourselves. We ask the question: What does it mean to love ourselves? This is a concept fraught with difficulties. Improper self-love translates into a lifestyle that is hedonistic, selfish, and self-destructive. But we dare not avoid the subject, because failing to love ourselves properly is also self-destructive. With low (or no) self-esteem, people become doormats for others, fail to use their Christ-given gifts, and have difficulty loving others. Jesus calls us to walk the narrow road between selfishness and selflessness. This involves a proper self-understanding, a larger dose of humility, and a healthy sense of who we are.

In the final book, we look at our relationship with other people. Christ's call is, at its root, a call to love others. Yet this is so often difficult. For one thing, others are not always very lovable; for another, loving them sometimes gets in the way of our self-interest. But we cannot avoid the issue. To follow Christ is to live a certain way. Behavior counts; lifestyle matters. But it's not all sacrifice and pain. Our greatest joys come from others. To be in a loving relationship with other people is to be alive and joyful.

A word to those who are not beginners on the way of Jesus:

So far, it would appear that these studies were written solely for the benefit of those who are new in the faith. In fact, they were written primarily for that purpose. But it's also true that those who have been on the way for some time need to be reminded of the fundamentals of the faith. Martin Luther stressed this to the clergy. He warned them against thinking that once they mastered the catechism (the statement of the fundamentals of the faith), they could then move beyond it. Instead, he urged them to recite the catechism daily as a spiritual discipline. He wrote:

> "As for myself, let me say that I, too, am a doctor and a preacher—yes, and as learned and experienced as any of those who act so high and mighty. Yet I do as a child who is being taught the Catechism…. I must still read and study the Catechism daily, yet I cannot master it as I wish, but must remain a child and pupil of the Catechism, and I do it gladly."[1]

There is something very powerful about remembering what lies at the heart of the faith. As Luther indicates, we can never master even the most fundamental facts. We need to be brought back to them constantly. In a real sense, we never get beyond the ABC's of the faith—nor should we. Thus, this series will be of value to the experienced Christian.

It is useful to have a study group that consists of both new and experienced Christians. Both benefit from the presence of the other. Both need each other in considering what it means to "learn to love." The older Christian brings experience and knowledge—years of seeking to know and live the faith, and this enriches new Christians. On the other hand, the new Christian brings freshness and wonder to this task—new eyes to see old facts in fresh ways, and so those who are older in the faith are reminded why they started on this journey in the first place.

Blessings on you as you seek to walk faithfully on the path to new life in Christ.

---

[1] Theodore G. Tappert, ed. and trans., *The Book of Concord* (Philadelphia: Fortress Press, 1959), page 359, quoted in Robin Maas and Gabriel O'Donnell, *Spiritual Traditions for the Contemporary Church* (Nashville: Abingdon Press, 1990), pages 167–168.

A Three-Part Program

There are three main sections to each chapter. Each section has a special function in the process of learning how to follow Jesus. Knowing the intention of each section will help you use that section to its full advantage:

- *Group Study:* contains materials for a 60- to 90-minute small group Bible study.
- *Study Resources:* contains notes and comments used in both group and personal study.
- *Personal Study:* contains a series of reflection questions for use by group members on their own during the week.

In turn, each of these three sections has various parts, which are discussed below.

Group Study

Small group Bible study is at the heart of this material. This is where you will learn, share, pray, laugh, cry, reflect, and grow—together with a small group of friends and fellow pilgrims. The Christian way was never meant to be a solitary way. It has always been a matter of community. The early Christian groups were not much larger than your small group. They met in homes, studying and worshiping together. It was not until the third century that special buildings were used for the gathering of Christians. So, in forming this small group, you are returning to the original way in which men and women learned to be disciples of Jesus.

Your small group study has several components:

❑ *Overview:* The first page of each chapter has a brief description of the topic to be studied and the materials that are presented in each of the three sections. This will give you a clear idea of what to expect and how to proceed. You will also know what results to strive for as a small group and in your personal study.

❑ *Beginning:* Each small group study will begin with a sharing exercise that puts you in touch with the issue that will be studied. This is a good way to begin a small group because it gets everyone talking. It helps to move you from what you were thinking about (or worried about) when you arrived at the meeting to what the text deals with. It also puts you in touch with the topic in an experiential way, so that your discussion is not just sharing ideas, but sharing your life. Most importantly, it allows you to share your stories with one another. The questions in this section always focus on life experiences, and they are generally fun to answer.

❑ *The Text:* The aim of the entire small group experience is to understand and apply a passage from the Bible to your life. You will study material from various parts of the Bible. Different translations will be used, so that you will become acquainted with the excellent variety of English language Bibles available today. Since the New Testament was written to be read aloud, you will begin your study by reading the text aloud. Words in bold type are explained in the *Bible Study Notes* section.

❑ *Understanding the Text:* Unless you notice carefully what the text says, you will not be able to interpret it accurately. The questions in this section are designed to help you focus on the key issues and assertions in the passage. You will also begin to wrestle with the meaning of the text. In this section, you concentrate on the passage in its original first-century context (in the case of New Testament passages). After someone in the group has read the passage aloud, take five minutes for silent study (in which you think about the answer to each question). The rest of the time is used for small group discussion based on the questions. Optional questions are provided for you to discuss as a group (when time permits), or for you to do as homework.

❑ *Applying the Text:* It is not enough to simply understand the passage. You need to apply that understanding to your own situation. This is the aim of the final section of the small group study. The questions in this section connect what you have read to how you should live.

Study Resources

The *LEARNING TO LOVE* series is enriched by various study resources that extend and expand both the small group study and your own personal study. Some groups will assign certain sections as homework to be completed in preparation for next week's small group. Other groups will assign these as follow-up materials to deepen the small group discussion. In all cases, maximum learning will occur if you take time each week to work through this material.

❑ *Bible Study Notes:* Assisting you in the study of the Bible is a series of notes that will give you the kind of information you need to make sense of the text: definitions of words, comments about cultural practices, background information from other books in the Bible, etc. In addition, each set of notes begins with some comments on how the passage you are studying fits into the unfolding argument or story in the book of the Bible where it is found (Setting). You will find entries in this section for those words and phrases in the text that are printed in bold type. The hope is that these comments will help to bring the text alive.

❑ *Comment:* This is a reflection on the meaning of the text. A key idea in the text will be highlighted, or there will be additional information about some aspect of the text. Sometimes connections are made between the text and your personal circumstances. This section is usually written by the author of the small group study; it may also include selections from the writings of other Christian authors.

Personal Study

❑ *The Art of Bible Study:* In each chapter, one particular aspect of the process of Bible study will be highlighted. The hope is that over the course of the twenty-one studies, you will become a proficient Bible student, able to understand and apply the text on your own. In *Learning to Love God,* the process of observation will be discussed. In *Learning to Love Ourselves,* the process of interpretation will be the focus. And in *Learning to Love Others,* the process of application will be highlighted.

❑ *Extra Reading:* Exploring the world of faith is exciting. It will lead you in many directions. The hope is that these studies will pinpoint the key issues involved in learning to live a life of faith. However, the studies can only introduce various topics. You may find that certain issues interest you, and you will want to explore these in more depth. The books listed here will guide your further exploration. Of course, you will not be able to read all the books listed; however, you should try to read some of them.

❑ *Reflection Questions:* Based on the text you have studied, certain questions will be asked to guide your personal reflections in this section. It is best used as a way to respond on a personal level to the insights that emerged in the small group study. Generally, there is no "right answer" to these questions— only the answer that expresses your own thoughts, feelings, and experience. Sometimes your response will be brief; other times it will be extensive.

❑ *Journal:* The process of journaling is a helpful exercise that promotes spiritual growth. You may not have enough room on this page for all of your thoughts, so you will probably have to let your writing flow over into another journal. In fact, you may want to put all of your reflections in a private journal (so you can freely express what you are thinking and feeling), and use this section to jot down notes about things to share with the group next week.

The Appendix

❑ *The Art of Leadership: Brief Reflections on How to Lead a Small Group:* Almost anyone can lead this small group Bible study successfully—provided they have some sense of how small groups operate and what the function of the small group leader is. This is the aim of this section. It provides a brief overview of how to lead the *LEARNING TO LOVE* small group.

❑ *Small Group Leader's Guide: Notes on Each Session:* In this section, detailed information is given for each small group session. The small group leader should review this material in preparation for each session.

Questions About the Study Guide

Since this book is not designed to be read by an individual on his or her own, but as a guide for small group and personal study, it is important to explain how it is intended to be used. The following questions will give some idea about the various possibilities that exist for this material.

Who is this material designed for?

▶ New Christians who want to learn what it means to follow Jesus as his disciple

▶ All Christians who want to review the fundamentals of the faith

▶ Interested seekers who want to explore the Christian way

What is it about?

▶ What is involved in being a follower of Jesus:
  • How one meets and knows God
  • The spiritual disciplines of Bible study, prayer, and worship
  • What it means to be a spiritual pilgrim, walking in the way of God

▶ Growing and nurturing the Christian life

What are the distinctive features of this series?

▶ These are spelled out in *What It's All About: An Introduction to the Series* and in *How It Works: A Three-Part Program.*

How do I form a group?

▶ Invite a group of (up to) twelve people to your house.

▶ Start with a potluck supper.

▶ After supper, explain the nature of the course.

▶ Give a study guide to each person.

▶ Then do the first session together.

▶ Agree to meet together for six more sessions.

Why should I belong to a group?

▶ It will help you to mature in your Christian life.

▶ Everyone needs the support of others in growing spiritually.

▶ This is a great way to get to know others who are on your wavelength in taking the spiritual side of life seriously.

▶ It's fun!

What if I don't know much about the Bible?

▶ This is the purpose of the small group: to learn more about the Bible together.

▶ The *Bible Study Notes* will increase your understanding of the Bible.

▶ The *Art of Bible Study* will help you to learn how to study the Bible.

▶ In any case, this is a small group for learners (not experts).

Can a church run these sessions?

▶ Sure! This material can be used in many different ways:
  • with new Christians   • in a new member's class
  • in a Sunday school class   • at a weekend retreat
  • in one-on-one discipling

▶ Either the church staff or lay leadership can organize it.

How often should we meet?
- ▶ Once a week is best.
- ▶ Once every other week works well, too.
- ▶ Do all the sessions at two consecutive Saturday seminars (9:00 a.m.–1:00 p.m.).
- ▶ Or do all seven sessions at a weekend retreat.

How long should we meet?
- ▶ You need at least an hour per session.
- ▶ Ninety minutes is best—this gives time for more discussion.
- ▶ Some groups may want to meet for two hours:
  - • This would allow more time for sharing.
  - • Members could share from their *Journal* reflections.
  - • You could also give time for personal study.
  - • You could work through the *Study Resources*.

What if we only have 50 minutes?
- ▶ Take 15 minutes to do the Beginning section all together.
  - • You may have time for only two of the three questions.
- ▶ Then split up into sub-groups of four each for the Bible study.
- ▶ Reserve the last five minutes for the sub-groups to come back together.
  - • Then the leader can give a concluding summary.
  - • Or the sub-groups can report on what they learned.

Where should we meet?
- ▶ In a home is best (since everybody is comfortable in a home).
- ▶ But anywhere will work as long as:
  - • You can all sit around in a circle facing each other.

What do we do when we meet?
- ▶ Each small group session has three parts to it:
  - • *Beginning:* in which you share personal stories
  - • *Understanding the Text:* in which you dig into what the text means
  - • *Applying the Text:* in which you let the text speak to you personally

What if we don't have enough time to cover all this?
- ▶ Don't try to discuss all the questions (the leader will select the key ones).
- ▶ Break up into sub-groups of four to allow more interaction time for each person.
- ▶ Best of all: expand the time of each session from 60 to 90 minutes.

Will we have enough questions for a 90-minute discussion?
- ▶ Generally you will, but if you don't, you can use the *Optional Questions* and *Exercises.*
- ▶ The *Optional Questions* can also be assigned for homework.
- ▶ The advantage of more time is that the open-ended questions can be discussed more thoroughly.

Is homework necessary?
- ▶ No, the group can meet together with no prior preparation.
- ▶ Homework does extend and expand the personal impact of the Bible study.

What is the purpose of the *Reflection Questions?*
- ▶ To assist individuals in applying the material in a personal way
- ▶ To facilitate recollection of the past and how it affects present spiritual growth

Can *Journal* entries be shared with the group?
- ▶ Yes, as long as everyone knows ahead of time that this will be done.
- ▶ In this way, not only will people work on their *Journal* reflections during the week, but they can select what to share.

What role can sharing *Journal* entries play in the small group process?
- ▶ This is a great way to tell your story to others.
- ▶ This deepens the impact of each lesson by following up the next week with practical applications of the ideas that come from group members.
- ▶ This brings the group into our decisions to change, and it makes us accountable to the group in a healthy way.

Who leads the group?
- ▶ Anyone can lead the group. Prior to the meeting, he or she must be willing to spend an hour or so to go over all the materials and to read the *Small Group Leader's Notes* for that session.
- ▶ The role of the leader is to facilitate conversation, not to teach or counsel.
- ▶ Shared leadership is often good. In this way, no individual can begin to dominate the group.
- ▶ However, certain people seem to be better at leading discussions than others, and they should probably be allowed to exercise this gift.
- ▶ Even in this case, it is a good idea to give new leaders experience in running the group so they can develop their skills.

GROUP COVENANT: every member should consider his or her responsibilities to the group and agree.

- ▶ **Attendance:** to be at the session each week, unless a genuine emergency arises
- ▶ **Participation:** to enter enthusiastically into the group discussion and sharing
- ▶ **Confidentiality:** not to share with anyone outside the group the stories of those in the group
- ▶ **Honesty:** to be forthright and truthful in what is said; if you do not feel you can share something, say "I pass" for that question
- ▶ **Openness:** to be candid with the others in appropriate ways
- ▶ **Respect:** not to judge others, give advice, or criticize
- ▶ **Care:** to be open to the needs of each other in appropriate ways

Chapter One
Encountering God

Faith begins with a conscious awareness of God. God ceases to be a mere concept which you believe or disbelieve; instead, God becomes a living reality who is known. This discovery that God is alive and personal happens in different ways for different people.

In this chapter, we will explore how one encounters God through a Bible study in which we examine Paul's conversion on the Damascus road (Acts 22:3–16); through an essay on different types of experiences of God; and by reflecting on how we have encountered God.

The hope is that through the small group experience and your own study, you will have a better understanding of how people encounter God and a clearer, sharper sense of the meaning of your own journey of faith.

Beginning *(20 minutes)*

Searching for God

People search for God in different ways. There is no "standard pattern" which defines this search. For some people, the search takes years; others find God in an instant. In your first session (after introductions), you will have the chance to share how you sought to know about God.

1. Introduce yourself to the group:
   - ▶ Briefly describe where you work (or what you do), and who your family is.
   - ▶ Give one reason why you came to this group.

2. People learn about God in different ways. Which of the following has been most meaningful to you in learning about God?
   - ❏ reading about God
   - ❏ going to church
   - ❏ learning from a wise teacher
   - ❏ reading the Bible
   - ❏ hearing about God from a friend/relative
   - ❏ meeting God when my life was falling apart
   - ❏ being challenged by someone to know God
   - ❏ joining a group
   - ❏ other: _____

3. What attracts you to God?
   - ❏ the need for meaning in my life
   - ❏ the hope of heaven
   - ❏ the desire to be forgiven
   - ❏ the need which God meets
   - ❏ the desire to follow what is true
   - ❏ the fear of hell
   - ❏ the need for faith
   - ❏ the sense of God's majesty

The Text

"I am a Jew, born in **Tarsus**[1] of Cilicia, but brought up in this city. Under **Gamaliel** I was thoroughly trained in the law of our fathers and was just as **zealous** for God as any of you are today. I persecuted the followers of this Way to their death, arresting both men and women and throwing them into prison, as also the high priest and all the Council can testify. I even obtained letters from them to their brothers in Damascus, and went there to bring these people as prisoners to Jerusalem to be punished.

"About noon as I came near Damascus, suddenly a **bright light** from heaven flashed around me. I fell to the ground and heard a voice say to me, '**Saul! Saul! Why do you persecute me?**'

" '**Who are you, Lord?**' I asked.

" 'I am **Jesus of Nazareth**, whom you are persecuting,' he replied.' My companions saw the light, but they did not understand the voice of him who was speaking to me.

" '**What shall I do, Lord?**' I asked.

" 'Get up,' the Lord said, 'and go into Damascus. There you will be told all that you have been assigned to do.' My companions led me by the hand into Damascus, because the brilliance of the light had blinded me.

"A man named **Ananias** came to see me. He was a devout observer of the law and highly respected by all the Jews living there. He stood beside me and said, 'Brother Saul, receive your sight!' And at that very moment I was able to see him.

"Then he said: 'The God of our fathers has chosen you to know his will and to see the Righteous One and to hear words from his mouth. You will be his **witness** to all men of what you have seen and heard. And now what are you waiting for? Get up, be **baptized** and wash your **sins** away, calling on his name.' "

Acts 22:3–16
New International Version[2]

Understanding the Text (20 minutes)

One of the most dramatic encounters with God happened to Saul, the Jewish leader who became Paul, the Christian apostle as a result of it. It was an experience that revolutionized Paul's life. He was, literally, never the same again. During his ministry as an apostle, Paul came back again and again to his encounter with Jesus on the Damascus Road—it was so important to him. The text we are going to study is the second of three times this encounter is told in the Acts of the Apostles. Paul is the one who is speaking in this passage.

1. List all the facts that Paul gives us about himself:
   - ▶ ethnic identity
   - ▶ education
   - ▶ activities
   - ▶ birthplace
   - ▶ attitude about life

2. Describe the encounter:
   - ▶ Where does it take place?
   - ▶ What does Paul see and hear?
   - ▶ Who does Paul encounter?
   - ▶ When does it happen?
   - ▶ What do his companions see and hear?
   - ▶ What does Paul do?

3. What was expected of Paul:
   - ▶ Immediately?
   - ▶ Long term?

4. Try to imagine what it would have been like for Paul to meet Ananias. What was Paul thinking and feeling? What would Ananias have been thinking and feeling?

Optional Questions

A surprisingly large number of Christians have had mystical experiences. These events are characterized by:

◆ an awareness that they are in touch with a supernatural presence
◆ a sense of power
◆ intense feelings of joy, bliss, awe, trust, ecstasy
◆ a conviction that there is more to reality than what we perceive with our five senses
◆ extraordinary phenomena such as heat, light, a voice, a sense of being touched—experiences not associated with their ordinary environments

All of these characteristics aren't present in every mystical experience: different people have different experiences. Some of these experiences are tranquil, some are intense. Yet all bring with them the feeling of the presence of the supernatural.

1. In what ways does Paul's experience fit this definition of a mystical experience? How does it differ?

2. Given what you know about Paul's background as a Jewish religious leader, discuss the assertion that the only way he could ever have been converted to Christianity was through a dramatic event like this.

Applying the Text (20 minutes)

1. From the information in this passage, how would you describe the kind of person Paul was? What moved and motivated him?

2. What is the nearest you have come to the sort of experience Paul had?
   ❑ an inner sense of God's presence
   ❑ a mystical experience
   ❑ a spine-tingling sense that somebody was there
   ❑ a deep longing for something (or someone) beyond
   ❑ a conversion experience
   ❑ a sense of call from God
   ❑ nothing quite like this
   ❑ other: _____

3. Briefly describe how you came to know that God was alive and real; or describe how you have been searching for God.

4. From this experience, what did Paul discover about himself? About God? What has your encounter with (or search for) God taught you about yourself? About God?

5. To which task did God call Paul? To which task has God called you?

Optional Questions

Read the *Comment* section on page 19. In it, the stories of five people are told.

1. Have you heard about an encounter with God that you can share with the group? If so, tell this story to the group.

2. With whose story—Joe's, Jane's, Jon's, David's, or Carrie's—do you most closely identify? Explain.

Bible Study Notes

Setting: It was this experience that turned Paul around from being a murderous Pharisee to becoming a tireless Apostle. This is the second of three accounts of his conversion in Acts (see also Acts 9:1–19 and 26:4–23).[3] This time, Paul tells the story to a hostile crowd at the temple in Jerusalem. It is his defense in light of his false arrest (for supposedly bringing a Gentile into the forbidden areas of the temple). He tries to explain the change that has taken place in his life.

Tarsus: The Roman city where Paul was born. It was a great center of learning in the first century.

Gamaliel: A famous rabbi. Since Paul studied under him, it meant that he was exposed to the finest possible theological education. Indeed, Paul emerges in these accounts as a man who was the epitome of Jewish spirituality.

zealous: Zeal was one of the most highly-prized attributes in first-century Judaism. You could pay no higher compliment to someone than to say that he was zealous for the law. Paul's zeal was demonstrated by his persecution of Christians.

bright light: In a mystical experience, it is not uncommon for there to be unusual sensory experiences: a bright light, a voice, an appearance. It's clear that something very unusual has taken place here: even though this occurs at noon (when the intense middle-east sun is brightest), Paul is blinded by an even brighter light.

Saul! Saul!: This is not a generalized experience with an impersonal "force." Paul encounters a person who knows his name and cares enough about him to stop him in his tracks on his murderous journey.

Why do you persecute me?: This simple question shines a light in the darkness of Paul's life. He learns a stunning truth about himself: he is persecuting God. Paul is not walking in God's way, as he had assumed. He is a killer, breaking the Sixth Commandment: "You shall not murder" (Exodus 20:13). This truth continued to haunt Paul for the rest of his life (1 Corinthians 15:9; Galatians 1:13,23; Philippians 3:6; 1 Timothy 1:13).

Who are you, Lord?: Paul does not know who, specifically, he is persecuting. Who is speaking on behalf of the Christians? The title, "Lord," indicates Paul's submission to the voice.

Jesus of Nazareth: This discovery (that Jesus was alive and empowered by God) must have overwhelmed Paul. It turned his assumptions about God (and God's will) upside down.

What shall I do, Lord?: Paul recognizes that this encounter demands a response. There is a new path to be followed.

Ananias: Ananias is not at all sure why God has chosen him for the task of welcoming Paul into the Christian community: "Lord," he responds when called by God to seek out Paul, "I have heard many reports about this man and the harm he has done to your saints in Jerusalem. And he has come here with authority from the chief priests to arrest all who call on your name!" (Acts 9:13–14). However, he is assured by the Lord: "Go! This man is my chosen instrument to carry my name before the Gentiles and their kings and before the people of Israel" (Acts 9:15).

witness: Paul's new role is to be a spokesman for God and for Jesus. At the heart of what he will share is his encounter with Jesus on the Damascus road.

baptized: In this way, Paul publicly identifies himself as a Christian.

sins: Sin is the issue. The specific sin in Paul's life (the one that reveals to him what he has become) is the sin of killing others—a clear contradiction of the Sixth Commandment. However, his murderous activity is just the outworking of a larger fact: he is, by nature (as are all people) a sinner, cut off from God and in need of God's forgiveness. To be baptized in the name of Jesus is to confess the fact of this sin, to ask for God's forgiveness, and to receive his forgiveness (which is made possible by the death of Christ on our behalf and in our place).

Comment

Encounters with God

It happens in different ways at different times with different people. But the core of the experience is the same: we encounter the Living God. Sometimes the experience is fleeting—a mere brush against the fabric of the divine. At other times, it is overwhelming—we touch a power we never knew existed, and we are filled with joy (while simultaneously filled with fear).

Consider the ways God meets us:

- It is 6:00 a.m. on a quiet lake in Maine. Joe is all alone in the canoe. The sun is barely up. As the mist rises off the water, the mountains are outlined against the sky. The stillness is overwhelming. Within Joe there is a yearning to be part of this perfection, this calm, this creation. It is a longing to penetrate, to be in touch with the Reality that lies behind this present reality. He wants to know the One who is creator of all that surrounds him.
- Jane's father dies—suddenly, without warning—his heart stops functioning. Her world is shattered. So much was left unsaid to her father, so much love left unexpressed. Now he is gone. And yet in her sobbing grief, there is another note: a sense of Presence, a chiming of Joy. She reaches out to claim it and is met by a new Reality.
- Jon always knew God—even though (as an adult) he dismissed his childhood experiences. But now he claims them again. He says "Yes" to the strong sense he had as a five-year-old that God loved him; he responds to the voice of God he heard as a little boy calling to him to be God's person. As Jon's heart acknowledges all this to be true, it is strangely warmed.
- For David, the sense of God's presence came without warning, without precedent. His children were pre-teens, in need of "moral education." As a responsible father, he first checked out the local church where he would send them. This is why he was in church on a Saturday afternoon at a special "Youth Rally." Sitting by himself in the back, hardly paying much attention to the service, he is suddenly overwhelmed by the presence of God. In an instant his life is turned around. One minute God was a concept he did not believe in, the next minute God is a Living Reality.
- Carrie thought her way to God. Possessed by a burning desire to know, she wrestled with issues of meaning. She investigated the concept of God. It was out of her slow, patient study of the Bible that she concluded that God was real, and that she could know God through Jesus.

Our experiences are so different:

- God's presence shines at us through his creation.
- Disaster rips our lives apart and shows us the true reality beneath it all.
- There is an intuitive sense of God in human beings.
- God reveals himself to us dramatically.
- We find God through our powers of reason.

This is hardly a complete list of experiences. God is real and alive, and he reveals himself to us in a host of ways. What we are called upon to do is to notice and respond.

The Art of Bible Study

The Power of Observation

All good Bible study begins by noticing the facts of the account. If we do not invest the time necessary to observe the details of the text, we will not be able to interpret the passage accurately.

It is not easy to notice the details of a passage. For one thing, most of us are lazy observers. We can't help it. We are bombarded daily with an overwhelming amount of data, most of which we tune out for our sanity's sake. But this also means that we tune out some of what we ought to take in. In addition, if we have a history of Bible reading, passages can become so familiar that we no longer see what they contain. In both cases, we need help in observation.

Reading a passage several times is the first step in noticing what is there. Read the passage over slowly. Read it a second time. Read it in a different translation.

Then start asking a series of questions of the passage. This is at the heart of the observation process: asking questions that force us to see what is there. There are six standard questions we ask: who, where, when, what, why, and how. (In the following two chapters you will see, specifically, how to use these words.)

It is important to write down our answers to these questions. The results of our observation will then become the material we work with in interpretation.

Example: See question 2 in the *Understanding the Text* section (page 16). Notice how questions are asked of the text. The *Understanding the Text* section always begins with observation questions.

Extra Reading

These books describe the variety of encounters between God and human beings:

♦ *Knowing the Face of God: The Search for a Personal Relationship with God,* by Tim Stafford (Zondervan). In this highly readable and very personal book, a well-known Christian writer describes his search for God. He spells out what it means to have a personal relationship with God.

♦ *Knowing God* by J. I. Packer (InterVarsity). A classic biblical and theological study of this key question.

♦ "The Supernatural," *Leadership* magazine, Volume XII, No. 3 (Spring 1991). This issue has a series of articles on the topic of how people know and experience the supernatural.

♦ *Voices From the Heart: Four Centuries of American Piety* edited by Roger Lundin and Mark A. Noll (Eerdmans). A collection of accounts by people (ranging from Jonathan Edwards to John Updike, Henri Nouwen, and Charles Colson) showing the range of religious experience.

♦ *Conversions: The Christian Experience* edited by Hugh T. Kerr and John Mulder (Eerdmans). A collection of accounts ranging from St. Augustine to

C.S. Lewis, Thomas Merton, and Malcolm Muggeridge (in which the authors describe the experience of conversion).

◆ *Experiencing God: Theology as Spirituality* by Kenneth Leech (Harper & Row). A somewhat weighty but highly-stimulating vision of what a renewed Christian spirituality might look like.

◆ *The Idea of the Holy* by Rudolf Otto (Penguin Books). A classic study of the nature of human encounter with God.

Reflection Questions

For your *Journal* exercise, ponder the question of how people meet God, focusing on your own experiences of God.

1. Recall the experiences you have had of God. Record what you remember of them. Reflect on how each experience affected you.

2. If you have never had a dramatic experience of God, how do you respond when you hear the stories of others who have had such experiences? Why?

3. Do you want a vivid, dramatic experience of God? Reflect on this question.

4. What has God called you to do? What has your response looked like? What do you think the future holds for you as you seek to be obedient to God?

5. What was the most powerful lesson for you from the story of Paul's conversion?

6. Address God. Write out a prayer that praises him for who he is, and responds to what he asks of you.[4]

---

[1] Words and phrases in bold type appear with comments and/or definitions in the *Bible Study Notes* section on page 18.

[2] Note that the passages studied are taken from various translations of the Bible. In this way, you will become acquainted with the excellent assortment of English Bibles available today.

[3] In these notes, cross references will be made from time to time to other passages in the Bible. If possible, look up these references (since they contain additional information, extend the text, or confirm what is in the passage). In the front of your Bible, you will find a list of abbreviations for the books of the Bible.

[4] From time to time, the masculine pronoun will be used to refer to God. God is neither male nor female, of course. God is personal, however, so the English language requires us to use gender language to express the personal. While the Bible often refers to God the Father, there are other places where God is referred to in feminine terms.

Journal

Chapter Two
Knowing God

Overview

It is one thing to encounter God; it is quite another to give one's life to God. While many people have experiences which are mystical in nature, not all enter into a relationship with the One whose life and power they have touched.

We will explore the process of knowing God through a Bible study in which we examine the conversion of the Philippian jailer and his family (Acts 16:25–34); through two essays on what it means to "believe in the Lord Jesus"; and by means of reflection on your own experience of faith in Jesus.

The hope is that through the small group experience and your own study, you will better understand your own experience of knowing God.

Beginning (20 minutes)

Early Glimpses of God

Most children are aware of God. At least this is the case until society pushes this intuitive sense of God out of their active consciousness. Still, our childhood experiences of God are important to us when, as adults, we seek to have a vital relationship with God. Some of those early images are accurate; some are wrong; all need to be reevaluated.

1. When you were a child, who was God to you?
   - ❑ a benevolent grandfather-figure
   - ❑ a frightening entity who was out to get me
   - ❑ a presence
   - ❑ a mythical being
   - ❑ someone I thought a lot about
   - ❑ someone I thought little about
   - ❑ something like "the Force" in *Star Wars*
   - ❑ no memories
   - ❑ other: _____

2. How did you relate to the God of your childhood?
   - ❑ obediently
   - ❑ disobediently
   - ❑ in fear
   - ❑ in love
   - ❑ not at all
   - ❑ other: _____

3. If a child asked you, "What is God like?" what one thing would you say?

The Text

About midnight **Paul** and **Silas** were praying and singing **hymns** to God, and the prisoners were listening to them, and suddenly there was a great earthquake, so that the foundations of the prison were shaken; and immediately all the doors were opened and everyone's **fetters** were unfastened. When the **jailer** woke and saw that the prison doors were open, he drew his sword and was about to kill himself, supposing that the prisoners had escaped. But Paul cried with a loud voice, "Do not harm yourself, for we are all here."

And he called for lights and rushed in, and trembling with fear he fell down before Paul and Silas, and brought them out and said, "Men, **what must I do to be saved**?"

And they said, "**Believe** in the **Lord** Jesus and you will be saved, you and your household." And they spoke the word of the Lord to him and to **all that were in his house**. And he took them the same hour of the night, and washed their wounds, and he was **baptized** at once, with all his family. Then he brought them up into his house, and set food before them; and he rejoiced with all his household that he had **believed in God**.

Acts 16:25–34
Revised Standard Version

Understanding the Text (20 minutes)

To love God, we must first come to know God. The key phrase is "come to know God." This is not something that happens automatically nor magically. Awareness and choice are both involved: awareness that God is alive and knowable through Jesus, and choice to follow God.

How we can know God is made clear in the story above taken from the Acts of the Apostles. The story begins when Paul and his traveling companion, Silas, stop over in a northern Greek town called Philippi. Here they get into trouble and are cast into prison. We pick up the story at this point.

1. Who are the people in this passage? Identify the seven individuals or groups named in this story.

2. Examine carefully the earthquake:
   ▶ At what time did this earthquake take place?
   ▶ What were Paul and Silas doing before the earthquake? The prisoners? The jailer and his household?
   ▶ What three effects did the earthquake have on the jail?

3. Examine the result of the earthquake:
   ▶ What was the jailer's first response?
   ▶ What was the jailer's reaction when he discovered that the prisoners were still there?

4. What was the jailer's first question? Paul and Silas' answer?

5. What two things did Paul and Silas do for the jailer and his family? What did the jailer do for them?

6. What is the final emotion which the jailer expresses? Why?

Optional Question

We do not act without a sense of need; we do not believe without knowledge; we do not experience change without commitment. Each of these took place in the lives of the Philippian jailer and his family. In what ways does your story parallel their story? Explain.

- ❏ I had a deep sense of need.
- ❏ I met a person who pointed me to Jesus.
- ❏ I followed the lead of my spouse (or other) who wanted to know God.
- ❏ I know about despair turning into joy.
- ❏ I learned about who Jesus is and that made all the difference.

Applying the Text (20 minutes)

1. How did Paul and Silas respond to the calamity of being tossed into prison? In comparison, how does the jailer react to his calamity? What do you suppose explains the difference in these reactions?

2. If you had been in this situation, how do you think you would have responded:
   - ▶ If you were one of the prisoners?   ▶ If you were the jailer?
   - ▶ If you were a member of the jailer's family?
   - ▶ If you were a Christian missionary like Paul and Silas?

3. A miracle has taken place. This is no ordinary earthquake: the doors open, the fetters fall off, but no one is hurt. This is no ordinary response: the prisoners do not flee and they express compassion for the jailer. The jailer knows that God is at work. He has probably heard Paul preach (since the town was not large). Now as the jailer realizes his need, Paul's words make sense: the jailer needs to know God.
   - ▶ The jailer's first response is to attempt suicide. What did this calamity reveal to him about his true situation as a human being?
   - ▶ What do each of the following crises reveal to people about their real needs?
     - ❏ the death of a parent
     - ❏ the loss of a business
     - ❏ the experience of an earthquake or hurricane
     - ❏ the breakup of a marriage
   - ▶ We do not come to God unless we realize that we need to come to God. When did you realize that you needed to know God? What happened?

4. The jailer asks: "What must I do to be saved?" This is the key question that all people need to ask.
   - ▶ What does the word "saved" mean?
   - ▶ What does the word "sin" mean?
   - ▶ What does it mean to be "saved from sin"?
   - ▶ How did you recognize your need to be "saved from sin"?

Optional Question

Read through the *Comment* section (on page 27) and answer the following questions:
- ▶ What does the phrase "believe in the Lord Jesus" mean to you?
- ▶ When and how did you come to "believe in the Lord Jesus"?
- ▶ What is your understanding today about who Jesus is?

Bible Study Notes

Setting: On this missionary trip, Paul and Silas journey to Europe for the first time. Their first stop is in Philippi, the key city in the district of Macedonia. While in Philippi, Paul and Silas were arrested for casting a demon out of a slave girl and thus ending her career as a fortune teller. They were beaten severely with rods and thrown into prison. The jailer was warned to guard them carefully, so he put them in an inner cell and fastened their feet in wooden stocks (see Acts 16:11–24).

Paul: Paul was a Jewish religious leader, a member of a strict religious order called the Pharisees, and an active persecutor of the church until his conversion while on the way to Damascus (see chapter one for this account). He then became the chief apostle to the Gentiles, starting churches throughout Asia and in Europe. He wrote many of the letters found in the New Testament.

Silas: Silas was the traveling companion of Paul on this missionary journey after Paul and Barnabas (Paul's companion on the first trip) decided to split up (over the issue of whether Barnabas' nephew Mark would accompany them—Acts 15:36–41).

hymns: Given the severe beating they had suffered, it was probably difficult for Paul and Silas to sleep. Rather than moaning and despairing, they remembered why they were in prison. They had been put there because of an act of kindness done in the name and power of God. Thus they prayed and sang hymns of praise to God, expressing their faith in God and their joy in the midst of suffering. The early Christians understood that they might be called upon to suffer for the name of Jesus. They also knew that joy could flourish in the midst of suffering (see Romans 5:3; James 1:2; and 1 Peter 5:6).

fetters: These were leg stocks which were very uncomfortable, since they forced the legs wide apart.

jailer: Probably an ex-Roman soldier, a man trained to obey authority in the strict atmosphere of the Roman army (where something like sleeping on duty was punishable by death). He feared the worst when he saw the open doors.

what must I do to be saved?: The jailer had apparently heard Paul and Silas preach. He knows that they have been proclaiming that men and woman could be saved from their sins by the death of Jesus. Having been confronted with the imminence of his own death, he is made aware of his need for salvation. Thus he desires to experience the salvation that Paul and Silas have been proclaiming. Salvation ("saved") is used here in reference to eternal salvation (and to the fact that by our sin, all men and women are cut off from the life of God). Our sin can be forgiven, however, and we can come back into a relationship with God. The source of our forgiveness is found in the death of Jesus. Jesus died in our place to pay the price for our sins.

believe: Paul and Silas indicate that the way a person claims salvation is by reaching out in faith to Jesus. The jailer must believe that Jesus died for his sin, and then ask Jesus for the gift of salvation.

Lord: A title of respect that indicates who Jesus is. The title carries with it the idea of authority. "Lord" was the official title of the Roman Emperors. In the Greek version of the Old Testament, it's the word used to translate the sacred name of God (Jehovah, Yahweh). So when Jesus is called Lord, it is a confession that he is the Messiah, God's anointed King. It is also a confession of his deity. He is God come-in-the-flesh.

all that were in his house: This included not only the jailer's family but the servants as well. They would be invited to reach out to Jesus in faith and to be baptized.

baptized: Baptism is the rite by which people declare that they are followers of Jesus.

believed in God: This is what brings such great joy to this man: he has come to faith in God, and it has changed his life.

Comment

"Believe in the Lord Jesus"

Notice that there are three parts to this key phrase in the passage: "**Believe in the Lord Jesus.**" First, we must "*believe.*" We have an intuitive sense of what the word "believe" means: to assert that something is true. Certainly "believe" has this meaning in the passage. However, what the Bible means by belief goes beyond cognitive affirmation. *Believe* also means "to put one's trust in something or someone." Because you hold certain facts to be true, you act on them. For example, you can say you *believe* that an airplane can carry you from Detroit to Los Angeles. But this is not belief in the full biblical sense until you get on that plane and trust your life to it. Second, the passage calls upon us to believe something quite specific. Belief as an end in itself is not being commended. We must believe in "*the Lord Jesus.*" We are called to believe one main thing: that the Lord Jesus, by his death, made it possible for us to be saved from our sin. Third, we are called upon to believe "*in*" the Lord Jesus:

> The Bible speaks of the man who "believes in the Son of God." There is a wide difference between *believing* a man and *believing in* a man. If we *believe* a man, we do no more than accept the fact that whatever statement he may be making at the moment is true. All that we are saying is that in a particular case we believe that he is telling the truth. If we *believe in* a man, we accept the whole man and all that he stands for in complete confidence and trust. We would not only be prepared to trust his spoken word; we would also be prepared to trust ourselves and our life to him. To believe in Jesus Christ is not simply to accept what He says as true; it is to commit all life into His hands and into His direction; it is to place ourselves in His hands in time and in eternity.[1]

Knowing Jesus who saves us from our sins   *by John R. W. Stott*

Supposing Jesus was the Son of God, is basic Christianity merely an acquiescence in this truth? No. Once persuaded of the deity of Christ's person, we must examine the nature of His work. For what purpose did He visit this world? The Biblical answer is "He came into the world to save sinners." Jesus of Nazareth is the heaven-sent Saviour whom we sinners need. We need to be forgiven and to be restored to fellowship with the all-holy God, from Whom our sins have separated us. We need to be set free from our selfishness and given strength to live up to our ideals. We need to learn to love one another, friend and foe alike. This is the meaning of "salvation." This is what Christ came to win for us by His death and resurrection.

Then is basic Christianity the belief that Jesus is the Son of God who came to be the Saviour of the world? No, it is not even that. To assent to Christ's divine person, to acknowledge man's need of salvation, and to believe in Christ's saving work are not enough. Christianity is not just a creed; it involves action. Our intellectual belief may be beyond criticism, but we must translate our beliefs into deeds.

What must we do, then? We must commit ourselves, heart and mind, soul and will, home and life, personally and unreservedly to Jesus Christ. We must humble ourselves before Him. We must trust in Him as our Saviour and submit to Him as our Lord; and then go on to take our place as faithful members of the Church and responsible citizens in the community.[2]

The Art of Bible Study

Noticing the Nouns

The first step in the process of observation involves noticing the setting of the account which you are studying. In particular, you want to make sure that you have identified the key nouns. You can do this by going through the passage and making three lists. In the first list, identify all the people in the passage; in the second list, note the place locations; and in the third list, note all the time references. Generate these lists by examining the passage and asking the following three questions:

▶ *Who* is involved? Make a list of all the people in the account. Include titles in your list. Make sure you know to whom each pronoun applies.

▶ *Where* does all this take place? List all geographical places. Also list any changes in location within the passage.

▶ *When* did this take place? Notice all the time references.

As you go through the passage each time, record your observations in sequence. If a name, place, or time is mentioned more than once, list the verse numbers of each occurrence next to it. In this way you will note repeated words. Repeated words are often the important words in a passage.

If you don't know whether to include an observation, put it in your list. Later on you will assess the significance of each observation.

These questions cause us to notice the setting of the passage we are studying. As we notice the setting, we should try to visualize it for ourselves. In this way, we make the words on the page come alive in our imagination.

> *Example:* See question 1 in the *Understanding the Text* section (page 24). This is typical of a "who" question, designed to help you notice all the people in the text.

Extra Reading

These books describe the way in which we come to know God:

◆ *Becoming a Christian* by J. R. W. Stott (InterVarsity). A booklet containing a concise, clear statement by an Anglican minister of what a person must do to become a Christian (including comments on the cost of taking such a step).

◆ *Basic Christianity* by J. R. W. Stott (InterVarsity). A greatly expanded version of the above booklet, extremely well written. *Basic Christianity* describes who Jesus is (arguing persuasively from historical evidence that he is the Son of God who rose from the dead), why we need to commit our lives to him (clarifying the fact and consequences of sin), how the death of Jesus saves us, and how to commit our lives to Jesus.

◆ *Why I Believe in Christ* by Charles Colson (InterVarsity). A very interesting booklet describing how the author came to faith in Christ.

◆ *Have You Considered Him?* by Wilbur Smith (InterVarsity). Another booklet, focusing on who Jesus is.

◆ *Mere Christianity* by C. S. Lewis (Macmillan). A penetrating analysis—intensely practical and highly readable—written in non-theological language. Countless men and women have become followers of Jesus as the result of reading this book, written by an eminent professor of Medieval and Renaissance literature at Cambridge University.

◆ *Introducing Jesus* by Peter Scazzero (InterVarsity). This is a book about sharing Jesus with others. It includes six Bible studies. As we seek to tell others about Jesus, our own faith is clarified and focused.

◆ *Meeting Jesus* by James W. Sire (Harold Shaw Publishers). Thirteen Bible studies on the life of Jesus, designed to introduce him to us.

◆ *What Makes a Man a Christian?* by Timothy Dudley-Smith (Hodder & Stoughton). This out-of-print book is well worth searching for. This is not an ordinary text, but a "programmed paperback" that allows the reader to ask the questions he or she has about the process of finding faith in Jesus.

Reflection Questions

There are several crucial words in the response of Paul and Silas to the Philippian jailer: words that change lives. In your *Journal* exercises this week, reflect on the meaning of these words.

1. Read the passage and the *Bible Study Notes* once again. Recall the conversation in your small group. Reread the *Comment* section. Then write your own definition of each of the following words. End each definition by personalizing the concept (i.e., what does it mean for you to be saved, to have faith, and to be committed to Jesus?).

   ▶ Saved (save, salvation)

   ▶ Believe (belief, faith)

   ▶ Lord Jesus Christ

2. The jailer asks, "What must I do to be saved?" "Saved from what?" we ask. A man needing to be "saved" is in some sort of trouble. In the ultimate sense, the Philippian jailer needed to be saved from his sin. Because of his sin, he was cut off from God. He couldn't know God. His sin was a barrier to knowing God, who is pure and without sin. (The Apostle Paul explains the idea of sin more fully in Ephesians 2:1–10.)

   What about you? In what ways does your sinful nature express itself? How did you come to recognize your need of salvation?

---

[1] *The Letters of John and Jude (The Daily Study Bible)*, translated and interpreted by William Barclay (Philadelphia: Westminster, 1961), page 133. Used by permission.

[2] From *Basic Christianity* by John R. W. Stott, (Downers Grove: InterVarsity), page 8.

Journal

Chapter Three
Being Sure We Know God

Do we or don't we have a relationship with Jesus? This is the question that sometimes haunts new Christians. It is not an inappropriate question. We want to be in a right relationship with God. We need assurance that we are his children. We are grateful that the New Testament gives us the assurance we crave. It declares that when we accept Jesus by believing in him, we have, indeed, become children of God. We need to learn to rest in this assurance.

We will explore the question of Christian assurance through a Bible study in which we examine two questions: "How do I know if I have really committed my life to Jesus?" (John 1:10–13), and "How do I know I will always continue to be in relationship to Jesus?" (Romans 8:35–39); through an essay entitled "Resting in Jesus"; and by means of reflection on your personal assurance of salvation.

The hope is that through the small group experience and your own study, you will grow in your assurance of salvation.

Beginning (20 minutes)

Awareness of God

To be a Christian is to be aware of following Jesus. Despite how we came to God, we are aware that we have done so. This awareness comes in different ways. For some, it's simply a matter of asking the question, "Am I a follower of Jesus?" that provokes the realization that indeed they are. For others, it is a realization (over time) that they are indeed seeking to do God's will, because following Jesus is what lies at the heart of their lives. For still others, there is no doubt that they know God, since the experience of coming to Jesus is so vivid and powerful for them that they can never doubt it.

1. When did God become more than a word to you?

2. In what ways are you most aware of God?
   - ❏ through how I feel
   - ❏ through how I think
   - ❏ through what I do
   - ❏ through worship
   - ❏ through prayer
   - ❏ through reading the Bible
   - ❏ through an inner sense of his presence
   - ❏ through reflecting on nature
   - ❏ through music, art, etc.
   - ❏ other: _____

3. Share one recent experience in which you were aware of God's presence.

The Texts

Jesus **came into the world**—the world He had **created**—and the world failed to recognize Him. He came into His own creation, and **His own people** would not accept Him. Yet wherever men did **accept Him** He gave them the power to become **sons of God**. These were the men who truly believed in Him, and their **birth** depended not on the **course of nature** nor on any **impulse or plan of man**, but on God.

John 1:10–13
J. B. Phillips: The New Testament in Modern English

Who shall separate us from the love of Christ? Shall trouble or hardship or persecution or famine or nakedness or danger or sword? **As it is written**:
     "For your sake we face death all day long;
         we are considered as sheep to be slaughtered."
No, in all these things we are **more than conquerors** through him who loved us. For I am convinced that neither **death** nor **life**, neither **angels nor demons**, neither the **present nor the future**, nor any powers, neither **height nor depth**, nor anything else in all creation, will be able to separate us from **the love of God** that is **in Christ Jesus** our Lord.

Romans 8:35–39
New International Version

Understanding the Text (20 minutes)

Two fears haunt new Christians as they consider their relationship to Jesus. As they look back into the past, the questions they ask are: Have I really committed my life to Jesus? Did I do it right? Am I truly a Christian? This issue is especially acute when the "feeling" that is sometimes associated with conversion vanishes. The answer to these questions is found in the passage from the Gospel of John.

Another question arises when new believers look to the future. They ask: What is there to prevent me from losing what I now have? Can anything take God's love from me? If so, what? How can I be assured of continuing my relationship with Jesus? The answer to these questions is found in the passage from Romans.

1. Examine John 1:10–13 by answering the following observation questions:
   ▶ Where did Jesus come to? By implication, where did he come from?
   ▶ What sort of relationship did Jesus have to the world—even before he came?
   ▶ How did the world greet Jesus?
   ▶ What happens to the person who accepts Jesus?
   ▶ To accept Jesus, what must a person do?
   ▶ Upon whom does this new birth depend?
   ▶ Upon what does this new birth not depend?

2. Now reflect on your observations by answering the following questions:
   ▶ What do you remember about the birth of Jesus in Bethlehem? What strikes you as the most amazing thing about the coming of Jesus?
   ▶ What do you think it meant for the Creator to become a creature living in his own creation?
   ▶ Why do you suppose that people neither recognized their Creator nor accepted Jesus when he came? How would you recognize God if he came into your group?
   ▶ What is involved in "accepting Jesus"?

3. Now turn your attention to the passage from Romans:
   ▶ List the seventeen "enemies" identified here that might be able to separate the believer from the love of Christ.
   ▶ In what ways could each of these stand between children of God and the love of God? In what ways are all of these experiences similar?

4. What does it mean to be "more than conquerors"?

Optional Question

What other fears (than the fear we have not actually come to Christ, and the fear that we may lose our salvation) afflict us as we follow Jesus? How might we deal with them, based on the way the above two fears have been dealt with?

Applying the Text (20 minutes)

1. Even today, people neither recognize nor accept Jesus. Why not?
   ❐ They find it hard to believe that God could become a human being.
   ❐ They know that accepting Jesus will result in changes which they do not want to make in the way they live.
   ❐ They have never been exposed to the good news about Jesus.
   ❐ They refuse to believe Jesus could be who he claimed to be.
   ❐ They are not tuned into spiritual questions.
   ❐ other: _____.

2. Which (if any) of the issues in question 1 did you have to deal with? How did you resolve the issue?

3. What does the concept of "new birth" mean to you?

4. If our new birth depends solely on God, what does this imply when we do not "feel" much like a child of God? What is the proper role of feelings in our religious life?

5. Which of the "enemies" (from Paul's list in Romans 8) poses the greatest threat to your faith? Why?

6. In what ways have you experienced being "more than a conqueror"?

7. How do you know you are a Christian, and that you are secure in the love of God?

Optional Questions

1. Turn to the *Reflection Questions* (page 37) and use question 3 to continue your discussion of the role of feelings in the religious life.

2. Where are you when it comes to "assurance of salvation"? If the issue is settled for you, describe when and how this took place. If you are still wrestling with the issue, what prayer do you need to pray in light of this struggle (i.e., what do you want God to do in your life)?

Bible Study Notes

John 1:10–13

Setting: These verses are taken from the introduction to John's Gospel (John 1:1–18). Here God's plan for the universe is laid out: Jesus, who is the Word of God (verses 1,14) and God's only Son (verses 14,18), becomes a human being and draws those who accept him into the family of God.

came into the world: A momentous event took place some two thousand years ago: God visited this planet. He sent his Son, Jesus, down through space and time to be born as a little baby in a stable in Bethlehem. To be sure, God had communicated with the people on this planet prior to this event. He did so through visions and dreams, by the words he inspired prophets to speak, by means of his messengers (angels), through the sacred writing he inspired (the Bible), and occasionally, he appeared himself. But in Jesus he came to dwell on this planet for more than thirty years, during which time Jesus taught, gathered disciples, healed people, and then died on the cross for the sins of humankind. Finally, Jesus even conquered death, and today he reigns over the universe in sovereign power. The name theologians give to the coming of Jesus is the Incarnation.

created: Jesus was a human being in every way. The ancient creeds stress that he was "fully man." But he was also divine and, as such, creator of the universe.

His own people: The immediate reference is to the Jews. Jesus was a Jew. In the broader sense, the reference is to people in general. Jesus came in the common flesh of all humanity.

accept Him: To accept Jesus means to open one's life to him. It is to believe in him in the way described in chapter two of this study.

sons of God: This is, of course, generic use of language which was characteristic of when the New Testament was written. Today we would say "sons or daughters."

birth: John uses the metaphor of "new birth" to describe how a person becomes a member of the family of God. Persons move from the world of the senses to the world of the supernatural when they are "reborn" in Christ.

course of nature…impulse or plan of man: Only God can give people a second birth.

Romans 8:35–39

Setting: Romans 8:28–39 is the conclusion and climax of Paul's description in Romans 5–8 of the great privileges of the children of God. He ends this section with five unanswerable questions (verses 31–35) which show the eternal security of God's people. We will examine the final, rhetorical question: Who can separate us from the love of Christ? The answer, as Paul shows, is "nobody and nothing."

Who shall separate us: Here (and in verses 38 and 39) Paul names all the enemies that might appear powerful enough to separate believers from the love of Christ.

As it is written: Suffering is not new. Paul quotes Psalm 44:22, which states that God's people have always been exposed to the risk of death.

more than conquerors: Through these experiences the believer is shown to be strong, indeed. This phrase means, literally, "hyper-conquerors" or "super-conquerors."

death: Even death, the ultimate enemy, cannot wrest a believer away from God.

life: Life is used here in the sense of distractions or calamities that lure people away from God.

angels nor demons: Neither benevolent nor malevolent spiritual powers are to be feared.

present nor the future: Nor can time separate us from God.

height nor depth: Neither can space separate us from God. This may be a reference to astrology and the spirits that were thought to rule above and below the sky. Or it may mean that neither heaven nor hell can separate a Christian from the love of God.

the love of God: This is the focus of the passage. It is God's love that is our eternal experience.

in Christ Jesus: The love of God is expressed in, through, and by Christ Jesus. It is by coming to Christ in faith that we know and experience, now and forever, the love of God.

Comment

Resting in Jesus

The pattern goes like this. A person becomes a follower of Jesus and is elated. All of life seems to take on new meaning. But then one morning, this new Christian wakes up and realizes with a start that the "feeling" is gone. "What happened?" she asks. She begins to wonder if she ever really was a Christian.

What about this? Can we expect always to "feel" the presence of God? Does our assurance that we are Christians rest on such a feeling?

In fact, we do not always feel much like a child of God. Our feelings are swayed by so many things in life—illness (who feels holy when suffering from stomach flu?), unexpected reversals in the economy (that generate worry about financial survival), relationships which go sour (when a friend deserts us, we wonder if we are unlovable), the weather (which makes us joyful or depressed), etc. It certainly is good, therefore, that the reality of our salvation does not depend upon how we feel about it. In fact, as the New Testament makes plain, our new birth depends exclusively upon the gracious action of God.

So if you have believed in Christ, you are a child of God. This is a fact to be believed because it is a fact taught in Scripture. You may not always "feel" that you are a child of God, but, as John 1 teaches, it is not your "feelings" upon which your rebirth depends. So when you doubt whether you are really a Christian, read this passage until its truth sinks in. Then believe what it says— a person is a child of God if he or she believes in Christ. This is a fact to be remembered, trusted, and depended upon in times of discouragement.

Consider the comments of various people of faith from ages past:

◆ To be assured of our salvation is no arrogant stoutness; it is our faith. It is no pride; it is our devotion. It is no presumption; it is God's promise.

Saint Augustine

◆ Our hope is not hung upon such an untrusted thread as, "I imagine so," or "It is likely"; but the cable, the strong rope of our fastened anchor, is the oath and promise of Him who is eternal verity. Our salvation is fastened with God's own hand and Christ's own strength, to the strong stake of God's unchangeable nature.

Rutherford's Letters, 1637

◆ Never did a believer in Jesus Christ die or drown in his voyage to heaven. They will all be found safe and sound with the Lamb on Mount Zion. Christ loseth none of them; yea, nothing of them (John 6:39). Not a bone of a believer is to be seen on the field of battle. They are all more than conquerors through Him that loved them.

Rev. Robert Traill, 1696 (English Puritan)

◆ This certainty of our salvation, spoken of by Paul, rehearsed by Peter, and mentioned by David (Psalm 4:7), is that special fruit of faith, which breedeth spiritual joy and inward peace, which passeth all understanding.

Rev. Richard Greenham, 1612 (Puritan)

The Art of Bible Study

Noticing the Action

The second step in the process of observation involves identifying the action that takes place within the text. You have already analyzed the setting (by identifying the nouns), so you are ready to analyze the action (by identifying the verbs). You can do this by going through the passage and writing down your observations based on the following three questions:

▶ *What* happened? List all the events in sequence. Do this as if you had a camera to take snapshots of the unfolding action. What happens first? Express it in a brief phrase. What happens next? And next? And so on.

▶ *How* does the action unfold? This particular question forces us to notice the sequence of events or the logic of the ideas. It is similar to the *What* question, but focuses on cause and effect.

▶ *Why* does all this happen? The *Why* question focuses on the meaning of the passage. Sometimes the author expresses the meaning of the passage himself, and it is our task simply to note it. Generally, we have to work at finding the meaning.

Action is clearest in narrative (story) passages. However, even in didactic (teaching) passages, there is movement from point to point. In the example below, notice how the text in John 1:10–13 unfolds step by step.

> **Example:** In the John 1 passage, the list of actions (the answer to the "What happened" question) would be:
> ▶ Jesus came.
> ▶ Jesus was not recognized.
> ▶ Jesus was not accepted.
> ▶ Accepting Jesus makes a person a child of God.
> ▶ Accepting Jesus means believing in him.
> ▶ New birth depends on God.

Extra Reading

Theologians call the topic we have been discussing "the doctrine of assurance" or "the perseverance of the saints." Not much has been written on this subject in recent years, so you will have to search a bit for information.

◆ *Christian Basics* by John Stott (Baker). Chapter 2 is entitled "How to be Sure you are a Christian" (pages 27–37). As usual, Stott writes with clarity and accuracy. This is an excellent place to begin your study of this topic.

◆ *Holiness* by Bishop J. C. Ryle (Kregel). An older book, but with a classic chapter entitled "Assurance" with many references to seventeenth- century Puritan writers (some of whom are quoted in the *Comment* section).

◆ *Christian Assurance* by Michael Griffiths (InterVarsity). A short book that warns the presumptuous against a false assurance, and encourages the doubter to realize the basis for his or her relationship with God.

◆ *New Dictionary of Theology* (InterVarsity). Check out the articles on "assurance" and "perseverance" in this (or another) good dictionary of theology.

There is another side to this question. We lack assurance because we have unresolved doubts. You need to investigate doubt. The following books will help in this regard:

◆ *Doubt* by Alister McGrath (Zondervan). This books deals with specific doubts.

◆ *Know Why You Believe* by Paul Little (Victor). Little discusses the basic questions which people ask about Christianity.

◆ *In Two Minds: The Dilemma of Doubt & How to Resolve It* by Os Guinness (InterVarsity). An excellent discussion of the dynamic of doubt.

Reflection Questions

1. What is the state of your inner assurance that you are a child of God?

2. Write into your *Journal* the following affirmation as a way of settling this question of your assurance of salvation:

   I *(fill in your name)* do truly believe in Jesus as my Savior and Lord. On the basis of the truth in John 1:10–13, I am, therefore, a child of God. I affirm that my salvation has nothing to do with me, and everything to do with the gracious work of God in Christ Jesus. This being the case, on this *(fill in the date)* I joyfully thank God for the fact that he has made me his child, and I rest wholeheartedly in this fact.

3. But what about the role of feelings in the Christian life? Use the following questions to guide your *Journal* reflections:
   ▶ What kinds of feelings did you have when you first became a Christian (or when you got serious about following God, or when you had a new experience of God)?
   ▶ How have your feelings changed (if they have)?
   ▶ What role do feelings play in your life in general?
   ▶ How can you value the feeling side of faith without being trapped by the need to feel something is true before you believe it?

Journal

Chapter Four
Learning About God

Knowing God is not a static experience; it is a growing relationship. It is vital to spend time nourishing this relationship. The remaining four chapters examine various aspects of growing a relationship with God, beginning with Bible study.

We will explore the question of learning about God through a Bible study in which we see how the Apostle Paul used the Bible as he sought to communicate to others the good news about Jesus (Acts 17:1–4), and then hear his description of the nature and use of the Bible in the life of Christians (2 Timothy 3:14–17); through an essay on the unique character of the Bible and its impact on the world; and by means of reflection on your own experience of the Bible.

The hope is that through the small group experience and your own study, you will grow in your excitement about Bible study.

Beginning (20 minutes)

Sunday School: The Good, the Bad, and the Ugly!

Many of us had some sort of religious education when we were children. For some, this was great fun and wonderful learning. For most, however, Sunday school (CCD, vacation Bible school, church camp—you fill in the blank) was a mixed blessing!

1. What sort of religious education (if any) were you exposed to as a child?

2. How well did it "take" in your life? Explain.
   - ❏ Not at all!
   - ❏ It made a deep impression on me.
   - ❏ It was fun but not educational.
   - ❏ boring teachers
   - ❏ great teachers
   - ❏ I was naughty.
   - ❏ I skipped out.
   - ❏ I tried hard.
   - ❏ I only went occasionally.
   - ❏ The person who taught me about religion was _____.
   - ❏ other: _____

3. What do you think is the best way to give religious education to children?

The Texts

When they had passed through Amphipolis and Apollonia, they came to **Thessalonica**, where there was a Jewish **synagogue**. As his custom was, Paul went into the synagogue, and on three **Sabbath** days he **reasoned** with them **from the Scriptures**, explaining and proving that **the Christ** had **to suffer and rise from the dead**. "This Jesus I am proclaiming to you is the Christ," he said. Some of the Jews were **persuaded** and joined Paul and Silas, as did a large number of **God-fearing Greeks** and not a few **prominent women**.

Acts 17:1–4
New International Version

Stick with what you learned and believed, sure of the integrity of **your teachers**— why, you took in the **sacred Scriptures** with your mother's milk! There's nothing like the written Word of God for showing you the way to salvation through faith in Christ Jesus. Every part of Scripture is **God-breathed** and **useful** one way or another—**showing us truth**, **exposing our rebellion**, **correcting our mistakes**, **training us to live God's way**. Through the Word we are put together and shaped up for the tasks God has for us.

2 Timothy 3:14–17
Eugene H. Peterson/The Message

Understanding the Text (20 minutes)

The Bible was central in Paul's ministry. He was an expert in the Old Testament, and used his knowledge of it to convince others that Jesus was the Messiah (as we see in the first text). He also urged Christians to devote themselves to learning what Scripture says (as we see in the second text).

1. Examine Acts 17:1–4 by answering the following observation questions:
   ▶ Where did Paul and Silas' journey take them? (If you can, consult a map in the back of a Bible and trace their journey.)
   ▶ Where did they go in Thessalonica? What did Paul do there (three things)? For how long? Who was his audience?
   ▶ What two facts did Paul seek to demonstrate? What conclusion about Jesus did he draw from these facts?
   ▶ What does Paul use as his authority in this dialogue?
   ▶ What is the outcome of his teaching and dialogue?

2. Why do you think Paul was so persuasive?

3. In what areas did Paul use the Bible authoritatively?

4. In your Bible, read about the conclusion of what happened in Thessalonica and about the trip to Berea (Acts 17:5–15). Contrast the reaction of the people in Berea to those in Thessalonica.

5. Examine 2 Timothy 3:14–17 and answer the following observation questions:
   ▶ What is the role of Scripture in our growth as Christians?
   ▶ What does Scripture do? How does salvation come?
   ▶ What is the source of Scripture?
   ▶ What four uses of Scripture are mentioned here?
   ▶ What does Scripture accomplish in the person of God?

Optional Questions

1. What role did the Bible play in your family when you were growing up?
   - ❏ We had a big family Bible.
   - ❏ It was read aloud to the family.
   - ❏ I didn't know what a Bible was.
   - ❏ We had lots of Bibles.
   - ❏ I had a children's Bible.
   - ❏ The Bible had no role.
   - ❏ other: _____

2. When, if ever, did you study the Bible? What was the circumstance (a college course, Sunday school, a Bible study, etc.)? What impact did this have on you?

Applying the Text (20 minutes)

1. How would you rate your biblical literacy?
   - ❐ I am pretty knowledgeable.
   - ❐ I have a good grasp of the NT.
   - ❐ I know some parts really well.
   - ❐ I understand the key ideas of the Bible.
   - ❐ I have read the Bible some.
   - ❐ I have a Sunday school knowledge of the Bible.
   - ❐ I am a beginning student.
   - ❐ I don't understand it.

2. How would you rate your habits of Bible study?
   - ❐ I study it almost daily.
   - ❐ I take courses about the Bible.
   - ❐ I read it from time to time.
   - ❐ I am just developing Bible reading habits.
   - ❐ I study it in spurts.
   - ❐ I read it regularly.
   - ❐ I never read it.
   - ❐ I don't read it a lot.

3. Given what Paul says about the nature of Scripture, what attention ought we to give the reading and study of the Bible in our lives? Why?

4. In what ways has Scripture:
   - ▶ shown you the truth?
   - ▶ corrected your mistakes?
   - ▶ exposed your rebellion?
   - ▶ trained you to live God's way?

Optional Questions

1. What is your goal when it comes to Bible reading? (check all that apply)
   - ❐ to understand the Bible better
   - ❐ to apply it directly to my life
   - ❐ to study it regularly
   - ❐ to become a knowledgeable Bible student
   - ❐ to draw strength from it
   - ❐ to fall in love with it
   - ❐ other: _____

2. Paul tells us that the Bible is "God-breathed." What is the significance of this fact to you?

Bible Study Notes

Acts 17:1–4

Setting: In chapter 2, we read about Paul and Silas in jail at Philippi. After their release they continued on, traveling southwest for about 100 miles to the city of Thessalonica.

Thessalonica: The chief city of Macedonia (the modern city of Saloniki in Greece). It stood astride a great international road.

synagogue: The Temple in Jerusalem was the only site for ritual sacrifice, but there were numerous synagogues throughout the Roman Empire. Each week the Jews met for worship and instruction. Visiting teachers were often invited to speak. Typically, Paul began his mission work in a city at the synagogue.

Sabbath: The special day set aside for worship of God (from sunset Friday to sunset Saturday).

reasoned: Paul sought to make clear what the Bible said about Jesus.

from the Scriptures: Paul would have used what we now call the Old Testament (OT). The Hebrew Scriptures were written over the course of hundreds of years. Paul based his argument on the source book that both he and his audience considered to be authoritative.

the Christ: Paul sought to prove that Jesus was the long-awaited Messiah ("Christ" is the Greek word for the Hebrew term "Messiah"). The OT prophesied that God would send the Messiah to rescue his people from their oppression. What the ancient Jews had not understood, however, was the way the Messiah would rescue them. They expected a military hero who would conquer their enemies. The Messiah came as a suffering servant to die for their sins (see Isaiah 53).

to suffer and rise from the dead: Jesus suffered and died on the cross (and so secured forgiveness for the sins of the world), and then was resurrected from the dead (and so brought new life to humanity).

persuaded: We are encouraged to use our minds as we come to faith. Paul probably urged his audience to consider that the OT foretold the specifics of Jesus' coming. He could also point to the fact that the impact of Christ's death on the cross is described in the Bible in a way that makes perfect sense (given God's ongoing dealings with humankind down through history). He could also argue that the resurrection of Jesus was a matter of history.

God-fearing Greeks: Many pious Greeks were attracted to the high morals and the monotheism of Judaism, and so they attended synagogues as proselytes (new converts).

prominent women: In NT times, women were considered second-class citizens. They were property owned by men. But Jesus treated women differently than his culture did. Many of his early disciples were women. Many leaders in the emerging church were women such as these.

2 Timothy 3:14–17

Setting: Paul urges Timothy to give heed to the Bible (which will lead him to salvation and which is central to his ministry).

your teachers: Paul reminds Timothy of the trustworthiness of those who taught him. Paul is probably referring to Timothy's mother Eunice and grandmother Lois (1 Timothy 1:5), who taught him the Bible when he was young.

sacred Scriptures: Literally, "the Sacred Writings," referring to the Hebrew Bible (OT).

God-breathed: Paul points to the divine origin and unique authority of the Bible. This is what it means when it is said that the Bible is "inspired."

useful: Scripture is helpful for the tasks of ministry—namely, teaching truth and showing people how to live.

showing us truth: The first use of Scripture is to teach us the truth of God.

exposing our rebellion: Not only does the Bible show us what is true, it exposes what is false.

correcting our mistakes: The Bible provides ethical instructions. It not only exposes error; it corrects wrong living.

training us to live God's way: The Bible not only corrects faults; it also shows us how to live.

Comment

The Bible

Consider the following facts about the Bible:

◆ It is the best-selling book of all time. More copies of the Bible are printed each year than any other book (over 100 million new Bibles or portions of the Bible). It has been translated into more languages and dialects (over a thousand) than any other book in history.

◆ It is considered one of the world's masterpieces of literature. It is beautifully written; it contains a wide variety of literary styles. Its ideas, words, and images are part of the very thought patterns of western civilization.

◆ It gave impetus to the scientific revolution by giving people confidence that there was a God-ordained order in the universe that could be discerned and trusted.

◆ It has inspired some of the world's great art, music, and literature.

◆ In the Epistle to the Romans, Paul single-handedly synthesized Greek and Hebrew thought—one of the great intellectual feats of history.

◆ It has become "America's book" in a way that finds no parallel in any other nation, influencing our literature (Melville's *Moby Dick*), poetry (Longfellow, Whitman), speeches (Lincoln's *Gettysburg Address*), drama (Archibald MacLeish's *J.B.*), popular fiction (James Michener's *The Source*), music ("Battle Hymn of the Republic"; Negro spirituals), and films (*Apocalypse Now*).

◆ It has influenced and guided great reform movements in history (such as the abolition of slavery and the role of women in society). It has influenced how we think about politics, economics, and law.

Why has the Bible had such a powerful, pervasive, and enduring impact? There are many ways to answer this question, but surely the underlying reason is that the Bible is the Word of God, God's self-revelation. The Bible contains truth about life and reality that we could not know by means of our own unaided reasoning. As such it has a special authority. The Bible acts as the final arbitrator of what is true. We shape our views (and our lives) to it—not the other way around.

This being the case, the Bible has a special place in the life of the Christian. It is where we go for accurate information about the way things really are, about who God is and what God intends for our world, about how we should live and what we should think. It is through the Bible that we come into personal contact with the Lord Jesus Christ.

But the Bible is not always easily understood. It was written over a long span of time in a variety of styles, addressing a host of issues (all by the guidance and inspiration of the Holy Spirit). As such, it is necessary to learn how to understand, interpret, and apply the Bible properly. The new Christian will want to develop the skill of perceptive Bible study. This is the intention of the *Art of Bible Study* section in each chapter. It is hoped that by the time you have worked through the twenty-one sessions in the series, you will be able to read and understand the Bible on your own. Equally important, the new Christian will want to develop the habit of Bible study. Christian saints down through the ages agree that regular Bible reading and meditation is central to growth in the Christian life.

The Art of Bible Study

Finding the Key Nouns

What are you supposed to do with the list of observations that you accumulate for a particular passage? Clearly, the lists are not ends in themselves. Who cares that a particular passage lists seven people, three places, and uses four kind of verbs? Bible study that only leads to observations is boring as well as useless. Observations are meant to lead us to interpretation.

In order to move from observation to interpretation, go back over the lists of raw data and reflect on what you have found. Begin with the nouns (the words which describe the setting of the passage):

> ▶ Make a new list in which you group together all the references to each person, place, and time. In other words, move from your list of raw data (which is recorded, in sequence, verse by verse) to a second list which collects together, out of sequence, all the references to each person (or place or time) in the passage.

Example: If Jesus is one of the names on the list, how often is he referred to in the passage? What other names or titles are used for him? Are there any phrases that describe him? Group all this data together under the heading "Jesus."

> ▶ Having done this, then make a third list which identifies the various types of people, places, and time references. Group similar people (or places or times) together into a "Cast of Characters," "List of Places," and "Calendar of Events."

Example: In the Gospels, you find different types of characters. There are the religious leaders (Pharisees, Sadducees, scribes, Herodians, Sanhedrin, etc.), the common people (noted by name or by characteristic: "sinners," "followers," etc.), the disciples (all together or by name), and the supernatural beings (God, Holy Spirit, angels, Satan, etc.). In any particular passage, you might find two or three of these types of characters.

Extra Reading

The nature, history, meaning, and characteristics of the Bible are subjects of endless fascination. Countless books have been written about the Bible. What follows are books that will help you study the Bible, and books about the Bible.

- ◆ *The New Revised Standard Version; The New English Bible; The Jerusalem Bible; The New International Version; The Message* (The New Testament in Contemporary English); *The New Testament in Modern English* (J. B. Phillips). These are examples of some of the best modern English translations of the Bible, samples of which are used in this series of Bible studies (so you can get a sense of each rendering). It is useful to have several translations for use in Bible study.
- ◆ *The NIV Study Bible* (Zondervan). You need a good study Bible (as well as different translations). This is one of the best—with excellent notes, fine maps and charts, and good introductions to each book.
- ◆ *Serendipity Bible for Groups* (Zondervan). Contains three types of study questions for each passage in the Bible. Useful for group or individual study.

◆ *The New Bible Commentary,* 2nd ed. (Tyndale House) and *The New Bible Dictionary,* 2nd ed. (Tyndale House). A single-volume Bible commentary gives you immediate access to the important issues in each book of the Bible. A single-volume Bible dictionary gives short descriptions of most biblical words. Both resources are *musts* for serious Bible study.

◆ *The Daily Study Bible* by William Barclay (The Westminster Press). There are numerous commentaries available for every book in the Bible. These provide more in-depth information than found in a one-volume commentary. (See *A Guide to Selecting and Using Bible Commentaries* by Douglas Stuart [Word] for a comprehensive list.) The seventeen-volume set of paperback commentaries on the New Testament by Barclay are noted for their clarity and for the interesting background information they provide for each passage. Barclay has the knack of distilling complex scholarly knowledge into simple, accurate statements.

◆ *The Complete Bible Study Took Kit* (InterVarsity). A user-friendly collection of materials to assist people in reading and applying the Bible.

◆ *Handbook for Bible Study* by Grant Osborne and Stephen Woodward (Baker). An introduction to the process of inductive Bible study.

◆ *How to Read the Bible for all Its Worth* by Gordon Fee & Douglas Stuart (Zondervan). An excellent introduction to the different types of literature in the Bible and how to interpret each.

◆ *The New Testament Documents: Are They Reliable?* by F. F. Bruce (Wm. B. Eerdmans) and *The Historical Reliability of the Gospels* by Craig Blomberg (InterVarsity). These books examine the New Testament and show it to be a reliable historical document which gives us accurate information.

◆ *Reflections on the Psalms* by C. S. Lewis (Harcourt, Brace, Jovanovich). A brilliant book on the Psalms and an example of the kind of books written about the Bible that illuminate and apply its meaning.

Reflection Questions

1. What role does the Bible actually play in your life now? What role would you like it to play?

2. What are your Bible study habits? How would you like these to change?

3. So far in this guide you have participated in four small group Bible studies. Reflect on the experience:
   ▶ What are the key lessons you have learned from the Bible so far?
   ▶ How has your attitude toward Bible study changed as a result of this small group experience?
   ▶ What are the best things about small group Bible study?
   ▶ How could you improve your small group Bible study?

4. What questions do you have about the Bible? How can you find answers to these questions?

5. It is clear that Scripture is meant to change us. According to Paul, it teaches us, corrects us, resets our paths, and trains us in righteousness. This is the reason we ought to read Scripture daily, so that our lives can constantly be changed for the better.

As you read the Bible this week, ask these questions (once you have observed and interpreted the passages):

▶ What does this passage teach me?
▶ How does this passage correct my ideas?
▶ What does the passage say about the direction my life should take?
▶ How does this passage seek to train me in righteousness?

Record your findings in your *Journal.*

Journal

Chapter Five
Conversing with God

Overview

Conversation is key to relationship. This is true in everyday life; it is also true in the spiritual life. To grow spiritually, we must be in conversation with God. Conversation with God is called prayer. The need of every Christian is to develop a significant prayer life. The nature and character of prayer is the subject of this chapter.

We will explore the question of conversing with God through a Bible study in which the group examines the most familiar of Jesus' prayers: the "Lord's Prayer," which Jesus gave us as a model of how to pray (Matthew 6:5–15); through an essay that explores the ambivalent relationship most people have to prayer; and by means of reflection on your own experience of prayer.

The hope is that by means of the small group experience and your own study, you will grow in your desire to pray.

Beginning (20 minutes)

Let Us Pray…

1. What prayer (if any) can you remember from childhood (like "Now I lay me down to sleep…," "Bless this food…," or "Our Father, who art in heaven…")? How and when did you pray this prayer?

2. When you were a teenager, what did you pray that your parents wouldn't find out about? What happened?

3. How do you usually respond to the prayers which your pastor prays during the worship service?
   ❏ Wow! Wish I could pray like that.
   ❏ Boring. I wish he would finish.
   ❏ Amazing. God loves us so much.
   ❏ Frustrating. I can't concentrate on the prayers.
   ❏ Thanks. Lord, you have blessed us.
   ❏ Other: _____

The Text

"And when you **pray**, do not imitate the **hypocrites**: they love to say their prayers standing up in the synagogues and at the street corners for people to see them. I tell you solemnly, they have had their reward. But when you pray, go to your private room and, when you have shut your door, pray to your Father who is in that secret place, and your Father who sees all that is done in secret will reward you.

"In your prayers do not **babble as the pagans do**, for they think that by using many words they will make themselves heard. Do not be like them; your Father knows what you need before you ask him. So you should pray like this:

> "**Our Father** in heaven,
> **may your name be held holy**,
> **your kingdom come**,
> **your will be done**,
> **on earth as in heaven.**
> **Give us today our daily bread.**
> And **forgive us** our **debts**,
> **as we have forgiven** those who are in debt to us.
> And **do not put us to the test**,
> **but save us** from the **evil one**.

Yes, if you forgive others their failings, your heavenly Father will forgive you yours; but if you do not forgive others, your Father will not forgive your failings either."

Matthew 6:5–15
New Jerusalem Bible

Understanding the Text (20 minutes)

Jesus was a person of prayer. He spent time in prayer (Mark 1:35–39). He prayed deep and meaningful prayers (John 17). Here in this passage, he teaches others how to pray. One of his disciples has just asked him: "Lord, teach us to pray, just as John taught his disciples" (Luke 11:2). This model prayer contains the key elements of prayer.

1. What is the "wrong way" to go about prayer?

2. What are the six verbs that define the six requests in this prayer? What is the difference between the first three requests and the last three requests?

3. Examine each phrase of the Lord's Prayer by answering the following observation questions:
   - ▶ To whom should we pray? What does this phrase tell us about God's nature and our relationship to him?
   - ▶ What does it mean for God's name to be "held holy"?
   - ▶ What are we asking when we pray:
     - "Your kingdom come"?
     - "Your will be done on earth as in heaven"?
   - ▶ What are we praying for when we ask for daily bread?
   - ▶ What is the connection between God's forgiveness and our forgiveness?
   - ▶ What is the meaning of the final prayer request with its negative and positive aspects?

4. Why do you think that Jesus connects God's forgiveness with our willingness to forgive others?

Optional Question

It seems that everybody has an opinion about the effectiveness of prayer. Some think it works; some think it doesn't. Some are agnostic about their prayers but know that when Aunt Judy prays, things happen. What about you?
▶ What is the most amazing answer to prayer you know about?
▶ Does prayer "work"? What do you think?

Applying the Text (20 minutes)

1. What motivates the "hypocrites" to pray? What should motivate us? What actually motivates you to pray?

2. If God already knows our needs before we pray, why is it necessary for us to pray?

3. Take each phrase in the Lord's Prayer and discuss what it means in relationship to the way you should pray:
   ▶ "Our Father": How do you acknowledge your relationship to God and your dependence on him in your prayers?
   ▶ "May your name be held holy": What things can and should you praise God for?
   ▶ "Your kingdom come": What is your part in the unfolding of God's kingdom, and how ought you to pray?
   ▶ "Your will be done": In what areas of your life should you pray that God's will be done?
   ▶ "Give us today our daily bread": What is the "bread" you need most to sustain you at this moment?
   ▶ "Forgive us": For which sins do you need forgiveness? Who do you need to forgive?
   ▶ "Do not put us to the test but save us": What are the tough areas in life from which you need deliverance?

Optional Exercise

The following themes are suggested by each phrase in the "Model Prayer."[1] Pick a theme and write out a prayer based on that theme. Then pray these prayers together as a group. Afterward, discuss the process of constructing prayers and how written prayers can benefit a person's prayer life.
   ◆ "Our Father": Dependence
   ◆ "In heaven": Affirmation
   ◆ "May your name be held holy": Blessing; Thanksgiving
   ◆ "Your kingdom come": Longing; Seeking; Doing; Serving; Peace
   ◆ "Your will be done": Dedication; Obedience
   ◆ "As in heaven": Guidance; Obedience
   ◆ "Give us today": Daily; Graces
   ◆ "Forgive us": Penitence
   ◆ "Do not put us to the test": Right living
   ◆ "Save us": Protection; Suffering; Compassion

Bible Study Notes

Setting: In Matthew 6:1–18 (in the "Sermon on the Mount"), Jesus focuses on the question of piety. He comments on three key aspects of Jewish religious observance: almsgiving (6:1–4), prayer (6:5–15), and fasting (6:16–18). In each case, Jesus first identifies a wrong way to go about such acts of devotion, and then he gives the right way. His point is that when "pious" acts are performed to be "seen of men," they are worthless. In the middle section, he discusses prayer and gives us the "Lord's Prayer." This is not only a prayer for use in Christian worship; it is also a model for how the individual should pray. The Lord's Prayer consists of three *petitions* directed toward God and his kingdom, and three *requests* that deal with the everyday needs of life.

pray: At various times during the day the pious Jew would recite prayers. If he had not arrived at the synagogue when the appointed hour came, that person would stop in the street and pray there. Apparently some people would make a point of being in a public place at prayer times.

hypocrites: This term comes from the theater and means "an actor." It is playing to an audience.

babble as the pagans do: "The eastern peoples had a habit of hypnotizing themselves by the endless repetition of one phrase or even one syllable. In 1 Kings 18:26 we read how the prophets of Baal cried out, 'O Baal hear us,' for the space of half a day" (Barclay).

Our Father: Prayer is directed not to some disembodied spirit, nor to some unknown entity. Christian prayer is directed to a personal God.

may your name be held holy: The first petition is that the name of God (i.e., his character and nature) be held in honor by all. In other translations, this phrase is "hallowed be your name."

your kingdom come: The second petition is that God establish quickly his promised kingdom, in which all will know him to be king. At present, his kingdom has been established in the hearts of his followers; but one day (at the Second Coming), the whole world will experience him as king.

your will be done: This is the third petition. This is not merely an acceptance of the inevitable. Christians pray this because they believe God's will is perfectly loving and righteous. They can, however, choose not to live within his will. Thus they pray they will remain in line with God's will.

on earth as it is in heaven: This qualifies each of the three requests: in heaven his name is honored, his kingdom has come, and his will is done. The essence of these three requests is the heartfelt desire for the same reality to prevail here on earth.

Give us today our daily bread: The first request is for the food necessary to sustain life on a day-by-day basis. In first-century Israel, finding enough to eat was the central preoccupation of each day for many people. By urging us to pray for our needs (great and small), Jesus reminds Christians that God is active in all of life. The prayer is for bread *today* (and not for "bread forever"), keeping the focus on the here-and-now, the daily provision by God. But the concern here is not just for food. In John 6:27–58, Jesus calls himself "the bread of life." Christians need spiritual (as well as physical) food in order to be sustained.

forgive us: The second request acknowledges that all people sin and need God's forgiveness.

debts: Both sins of commission (the wrong we have done) and sins of omission (the things we have left undone) are in view here. Humans beings are imperfect in what we think, feel, and do, and so are in need of constant forgiveness. Certainly this is a fact borne out by our daily experiences.

as we have forgiven: To pray for forgiveness without being willing to forgive others is an act of insincerity.

do not put us to the test, but save us: The third request (which has two parts to it) is that the one who prays will not have to face a trial so difficult that he or she will fail. We usually think of "tests" (or temptation) as "allurements on the side of pleasure which lead us into evil" (Plumptree). While the Greek word can mean that, it usually means "trials" or "trying circumstances," which is the sense in this prayer. Jesus prayed this type of prayer in the Garden of Gethsemane (Matthew 26:39). The request that God "save us from the evil one" points out who seeks to seduce people into evil acts.

the evil one: Satan, who is alive and active in this world. We ask to be delivered from the power of evil.

Comment

Prayer Is not Always Easy

Most of us approve of prayer. We think it's a fine thing to begin a meal with, or to open a new session of Congress. But very few of us, I suspect, whole-heartedly practice prayer in our own lives.

Part of our reticence to pray springs from misunderstanding. We are often taught that prayer is merely asking God for things. While asking is certainly a part of prayer (as the Lord's Prayer teaches), it is just a part. Rather, "prayer," as it has been said, "is a dialogue between two persons who love each other." It is not just asking a Cosmic Santa Claus (as some of us view God) for presents. Prayer is two people talking with each other.

We would pray far more if we were actually conscious that when we prayed, we were talking to a real, living person. More often, however, we feel our prayer is directed to a distant, somewhat disinterested Divine Being.

The next time you pray, start by saying, "Lord Jesus, I believe you are here with me now, wanting to converse with me." Then be still for a moment. Trust that he is present with you. Prayer becomes exciting when you realize that you are speaking to the living Christ. Then you can easily talk to him. You can share with him what has been troubling you. You can share what brings you joy, how much you love him, and anything else that makes up the fabric of your life. You can tell him the problems of others and ask him to help them. You can open your life to him to be changed for the better.

But prayer is not merely talking; it is also listening. Christ will speak to us if we listen. Sometimes we hear his voice through a passage of Scripture. Certain verses or phrases will have particular significance for us, and we will know that is God's word to us. Or we may hear his word through an idea which forces its way into our consciousness, and again we will realize that this is God speaking. One of the abilities we need to develop in our Christian life is discerning God's voice in the midst of all the other voices that crowd in upon us.

To get to know God and to grow in your love for him, you must enter into conversation with him. This is what prayer is all about.

As you undertake this study of prayer, here is a prayer to pray:

> O Thou by whom we come to God,
> The Life, the Truth, the Way,
> The path of prayer Thyself has trod;
> Lord, teach us how to pray!
> *James Montgomery*

The Art of Bible Study

Finding the Key Verbs

It is not just the setting of the passage that is important. In fact, sometimes the setting is incidental—a mere backdrop for the action or the ideas. So you must move from finding the key nouns to identifying the key verbs. (We will discuss how to identify key ideas in *Learning to Love Ourselves*). To find the key verbs, go back to your set of action snapshots ("What happened?"). Examine the verbs that you found. Ask:

▶ What kinds of verbs are present? For example, are the verbs indicatives (commands)? If so, what is the reader asked to do?

▶ What tense is used (past, present, or future)?

▶ Are the verbs active or passive?

▶ What is the main verb? In a passage with multiple verbs, it is necessary to find the verb that controls the action.

▶ In Greek, there is a more finely-tuned verb structure than in English. The newer English translations of the New Testament do a good job of capturing the sense of the Greek verbs. However, it is up to us to notice what is being said.

Knowing the right names for the verbs is not essential. Noticing the different aspects of the verbs (which you know just by comparing verbs) is the important thing.

> ***Example:*** See question 2 in *Understanding the Text*. The first three verbs are passive (imperative passives in the third person, to be exact). Literally: "Let be sanctified your name, let come your kingdom, let be done your will." They are responses to God. In contrast, the last three verbs are active (aorist imperatives in the second person). They are asking for something from God. The first three verbs have the sense of "let it be," in contrast to the last three verbs (which have the sense of "bring it about").

Extra Reading

You will want to read books about the process of prayer, books that help us to pray, and books that contain prayers.

◆ *The Oxford Book of Prayer* (Oxford). A rich collection of prayers drawn from a wide range of sources. As we pray these prayers, we are drawn into the piety of the ages—and we learn to pray in a deeper way.

◆ *Prayer: Finding the Heart's True Home* by Richard Foster (Harper SanFrancisco). Foster is a master at explaining clearly the nature of the spiritual life. Here he examines twenty-one types of prayer.

◆ *The Way of the Heart: Desert Spirituality and Contemporary Ministry* by Henri J. M. Nouwen (Seabury). A most compelling introduction to the spirituality of the Desert Fathers (and Mothers), with its emphasis on silence, solitude, and the prayer of the heart.

◆ *Prayer: Conversing with God* by Rosalind Rinker (Zondervan). A very refreshing and helpful book on prayer that is easy-reading. It also has a ring of reality that is most appealing.

- *A Diary of Private Prayer* by John Baillie (Charles Scribner's Sons). A prayer for each morning and evening, with the opposite page left blank for your own prayer requests. Highly recommended.
- *Letters to Malcolm: Chiefly on Prayer* by C. S. Lewis (Harcourt, Brace and World). "A book full of wisdom, of bitter honesty and of deep clarity. It nowhere tells us 'how to pray' but…stimulates afresh that hunger and thirst for God without which we should never pray at all," writes J. B. Phillips.
- *The Prayer Life of Jesus: Shout of Agony, Revelation of Love* by William & Aída Besançon Spencer (University Press of America).
- *Listening to the God who Speaks* by Klaus Bockmuehl (Helmers & Howard).
- *Rediscovering New Testament Prayer: Boldness and Blessing in the Name of Jesus* by John Koenig (HarperCollins).
- *Living in the Presence: Disciplines for the Spiritual Heart* by Tilden Edwards (HarperCollins). A series of prayer disciplines.

Reflection Questions

1. *When* we pray is important. Most of us need to set aside a definite time each day to pray. If we don't, we often find that the day has slipped by and we have spent no time in prayer. Set a time now when you will pray each day. Tell God when you plan to meet with him. Record here the time you have decided upon. *Where* we pray is also a consideration. We need a quiet place where we will be undisturbed. Where can you pray?

2. The Lord's Prayer is, for the most part, a petitionary prayer. It is about asking God for what we need and desire. The final three requests focus on our deepest needs.
   ▶ *Give:* We are invited to bring all of our requests to God, great and small. Reflect on what you need and desire.
     • What is your greatest need right now? Compose a prayer in which you bring this need to God.
     • How can you bring God more fully into the daily fabric of your life?
   ▶ *Forgive:* We need both to *give* and to *receive* forgiveness. On the one hand, we understand our need for forgiveness. Reflect on the areas in your life, past and present, in which you need forgiveness.
     • What are your chief "sins of commission" (what you do wrong)?
     • What are your chief "sins of omission" (what you have failed to do)? On the other hand, we do not always understand our need to forgive. But on more than one occasion, Jesus mentions lack of forgiveness as an obstacle which hinders our prayers. Reflect on who you need to forgive.
     • Who has sinned against you?
   ▶ *Deliver:*
     • Where are the struggles in your life?
     • What are the internal issues with which you struggle (depression, lust, laziness, anger, etc.) that you need to be kept from?

---

[1] These prayers are all taken from *The Oxford Book of Common Prayer*, section III, which contains prayers based on the themes in the Lord's Prayer. These are prayers number 166, 236, 341, and 394.

Journal

Chapter Six
Worshiping God

Overview

Learning to love God is not a solitary task. It is also a community experience—as we meet together with other men and women to express our shared love for God in worship. Worship of God has many parts to it. It involves learning about God, praising God, praying to God, celebrating the Lord's Supper together, as well as seeking to love other people in the name of God. Regular worship is vital to spiritual growth.

We will explore the question of worshiping God through a Bible study in which the group examines the community life of the first Christians (Acts 2:37–42); through an essay that discusses the nature and meaning of church, communion, and baptism; and by means of reflection on your own worship experiences.

The hope is that through the small group experience and your own study, you will grow in your understanding and experience of worship.

Beginning (20 minutes)

Going to Church

1. When you were young, what involvement did you have with a church, and how did you feel about it?
   - ❏ I attended church regularly.
   - ❏ I sometimes attended church.
   - ❏ I went to church only for weddings (funerals, etc.).
   - ❏ I went to church-sponsored activities.
   - ❏ I never attended church.
   - ❏ I drove by churches.
   - ❏ I knew kids who went to church.

2. What did you like best about church services? Why? What did you like least?
   - ❏ the hymns/the singing
   - ❏ the prayers
   - ❏ the music
   - ❏ the greetings by others
   - ❏ the sermon
   - ❏ the choir
   - ❏ the benediction
   - ❏ Communion
   - ❏ baptisms
   - ❏ nothing
   - ❏ everything

3. What means the most to you now in worship services?

The Text

Now when they heard this, they were cut to the heart, and said to **Peter** and to the other apostles, "Brothers, what should we do?"

Peter said to them, "**Repent**, and be **baptized** every one of you in the name of Jesus Christ so that **your sins may be forgiven**; and you will receive **the gift of the Holy Spirit**. For the promise is for you, for your children, and for **all who are far away**, everyone whom the Lord our God calls to him."

And he testified with many other arguments and exhorted them, saying, "Save yourselves from this corrupt generation." So those who welcomed his message were baptized, and that day about three thousand persons were added. They devoted themselves to **the apostles' teaching** and **fellowship**, to **the breaking of bread** and the **prayers**.

Acts 2:37–42
New Revised Standard Version

Understanding the Text (20 minutes)

The early church was a worshiping church. This is evident from the accounts in the Acts of the Apostles. We see this in the passage we are studying. It describes the aftermath of an extraordinary experience—the coming of the Holy Spirit. Three thousand people join the church that day. In describing this, Luke gives us a glimpse of how the church functioned in the first century.

1. Examine the text carefully by answering the following questions:
    ▶ What impact did Peter's sermon have on his hearers?
    ▶ What two things does Peter tell them to do?
    ▶ What two things will result if they do as he says?
    ▶ To whom is this promise extended?
    ▶ What was the first act of those who accepted Peter's message?

2. What does it mean to:
    ▶ repent?
    ▶ be baptized?
    ▶ receive the Holy Spirit?

3. What were four aspects of the life of the early church that these new believers experienced?

4. Scan Peter's sermon in Acts 2:14–36:
    ▶ What are its main points?
    ▶ What does he say to these pious Jews about who Jesus is?

Optional Exercise

Read the account of the coming of the Holy Spirit in Acts 2:1–13. Imagine that you are a pious Jew on a pilgrimage to Jerusalem to take part in a feast day. What would it have been like to witness these events? How would you have felt? What would you have thought? What would you have done?

Applying the Text (20 minutes)

1. In what ways was your response to the good news about Jesus similar to these devout Jews? Different?

2. In your church, what is the contemporary counterpart of:
   ▶ the apostles' teaching?
   ▶ fellowship?
   ▶ the breaking of bread?
   ▶ prayer?
   ▶ baptism?

3. Why is worship important for the individual Christian? For the Christian community?

4. Read the paragraph about Communion (in the *Comment* section, page 59):
   ▶ What is the meaning of the bread? The cup?
   ▶ Why do Christians celebrate Communion?
   ▶ What is the meaning of Communion to you?

5. Read the paragraph about baptism (in the *Comment* section):
   ▶ What does baptism symbolize?
   ▶ What does being "dead to sin" mean?
   ▶ What does baptism mean to you?

Optional Question

What role has worship played in your life in the past? Now? What role would you like it to have in the future?

Bible Study Notes

Setting: On the Day of Pentecost (a Jewish feast day), the apostles and other believers were gathered together in a room. They heard a sound like a violent wind. Then they were all filled with the Holy Spirit, and they began to speak in other tongues. A crowd of devout Jewish pilgrims who were in Jerusalem heard the sound and came to see what was happening. They were amazed to find a group of Galileans speaking to them in their native tongues (the pilgrims came from all over the Roman Empire). Peter addressed the crowd (preaching the first recorded Christian sermon) and explained what was happening. The Holy Spirit had come (as prophesied in the Old Testament book of Joel), poured out on the people by the power of the risen Christ from his throne in heaven. Peter ends his explanation by saying: "Therefore let all Israel be assured of this: God has made this Jesus, whom you crucified, both Lord and Christ" (see Acts 2:1–36). Our passage describes the response of the people to this sermon.

Peter: A fisherman from Galilee whom Jesus called to be one of the twelve Apostles. Peter quickly became the leader of the Apostles.

Repent: To repent is to change your mind about the way you have been living. It is to decide to stop following the way of sin and to start following the way of Jesus. When the decision to repent is coupled with trusting faith in Jesus, the result is conversion. William Barclay writes: "When repentance comes something happens for the future. We receive the gift of the Holy Spirit. Even if we repent, how are we to avoid making the same mistakes over and over again? There comes into our lives the power which is not our power, the power of the Holy Spirit, and in that power we can win the battles we never thought to win, and resist the things which by ourselves we would have been powerless to resist. In the moment of true repentance we are liberated from the estrangement and the fear of the past, and we are equipped to face the battles of the future."

baptized: John the Baptist (the one who announced Jesus' coming) had preached that people needed to be baptized for the forgiveness of their sins. This was highly unusual, since baptism was a rite required only of Gentiles who wanted to become Jews. Through baptism, Gentiles symbolically washed away their "gentileness." It was unheard of for Jews to be baptized. For the first Christians, baptism was a public sign that they had become followers of Jesus.

your sins may be forgiven: By his death on the cross, Jesus secured forgiveness for our sins. He paid the price for our sin. As believers are immersed in the water of baptism, they identify with the death of Jesus (and the washing away of their sins). As they come up out of the water, they identify with the resurrection of Jesus (and his gift of new life to them).

the gift of the Holy Spirit: When Jesus was about to depart from this world, he promised that the Holy Spirit would come and live in his followers (John 14:15–21,25–27). The Holy Spirit would be their counselor and helper who would stand by them. The Holy Spirit would lead them into the truth of God.

all who are far away: This is how Gentiles were spoken of. The extraordinary promise of forgiveness and the presence of the Holy Spirit was given not just to the Jews, but to all people.

the apostles' teaching: They would have taught what they learned from Jesus (Matthew 28:20). They would also have explained the Scriptures (the Old Testament) to them. In particular, they would have focused on the good news about Jesus' life, death, and resurrection.

fellowship: The early church was a strong community that met regularly in worship. In the early days, they shared all their possessions with one another so that no one was in need (Acts 2:44–45; 4:32–35).

the breaking of bread: Even though this phrase can refer to an ordinary meal, here (and elsewhere) it probably refers to sharing the Lord's Supper together.

prayers: Prayer to God was an important aspect of their life together.

The Church   *by John R. W. Stott*

The Christian life is not just our own private affair. If we have been born again into God's family, not only has He become our Father but every other Christian believer in the world, whatever his nation or denomination, has become our brother or sister in Christ. One of the commonest names for Christians in the New Testament is "brethren." This is a glorious truth. But it is no good supposing that membership in the universal Church of Christ is enough; we must belong to some local branch of it.

Every Christian's place is in a local church, sharing in its worship, its fellowship and its witness. Baptism is the way of entry into such a visible Christian society. It has other meanings as well, but, if you have not been baptized, you should ask your minister or chaplain to baptize you. Then do allow yourself to be drawn right into the Christian fellowship. Much may seem strange to you at first, but do not stand aside. Church attendance on Sundays is a definite Christian duty, and nearly every branch of the Christian Church agrees that the Lord's Supper or Holy Communion is the central service of the Church, for in it we commemorate our Saviour's death in fellowship with one another. I hope I am not giving the impression that fellowship is merely a Sunday treat! "Philadelphia," the love of the brethren, is a new word in the Christian's vocabulary, and he will discover new depths of friendship in the Christian brotherhood. His closest friends will inevitably be Christian.[1]

The Sacraments

We all need physical and tangible expressions of things we cannot see to help us know they are real. The love of a friend or a spouse, expressed in a simple gesture (such as a touch, a note, or a cup of coffee) assures us of the affection behind it. This is what the sacraments are. Literally, a sacrament is something sacred or holy which represents the hidden or mysterious. For Christians, the sacraments are the signs appointed by Christ that symbolize the covenant God has made with his people. They are outward and visible manifestations of inward and invisible realities.

Though Christians differ on the number of sacraments they observe, virtually all consider baptism and communion (the Lord's Supper, the Eucharist) to have been instituted by Christ himself and intended for all believers.

Baptism is, according to Romans 6:3–10, the symbolic dying to the former life of enslavement to sin by burial under the waters of baptism. It also represents the rising to the new life lived under the rule of grace, by the power of God. To the believer who undergoes it, baptism is both a public confession of faith and total commitment to Christ, and a permanent confirmation and reminder that he or she forever belongs to the Lord by his redemptive work on the cross.

Communion is the physical means by which God continues to apply his grace to our lives. When Christ shared his last meal with his disciples, he took bread, and after giving thanks, gave it to his disciples. He told them that it was his body, and that they should eat it in remembrance of him. He likewise gave them the cup, and said that it was the blood of the new covenant, poured out for many for the forgiveness of sins (see Matthew 26:26–29 and Luke 22:17–20). As we observe this sacrament, we are both reminded of and strengthened by the grace of our Lord—which was, is, and always will be the only foundation for our new relationship with him.

The Art of Bible Study

Understanding the Key Nouns

Once you have a clear idea of the key words in your passage, you then need to go back to the text and notice what is said there (if anything) about each of these important words.

For each of the key characters (places, times, actions), make another list in which you include everything the passage says about that person (place, time, action).

Example: In your text, the "desert" may be the key place. Does the text give any details about the desert? Is it called "hot," "dry," or "desolate"? What is the significance of the desert in the passage? These are the sort of questions you need to ask of each of the key nouns.

Once you have identified all of the data in the text you are studying, recall what the author said in previous passages about this place (person, time).

Example: Perhaps the desert has been the site of the temptation of Jesus, the preaching of Jesus, or a significant encounter with a person. In other words, recall what you already know about the place (person, time) from the author you are reading.

The objective is to use the *What* question to increase your understanding of the key ideas in the passage by asking: "What does the passage say about _____?"

Example: See question 4 in the **Understanding the Text** section (page 56).

Extra Reading

These books will help you understand more about worship, baptism, and communion. In the end, however, it is our understanding of worship that counts as much as participating in worship on a regular basis.

- ◆ *Signs of Wonder* by Robert Webber (Abbott Martyn). Dr. Webber has been involved in the worship renewal movement for over two decades. His other books on this subject include:
  - • *Worship Is a Verb*, Revised edition (Abbott Martyn). A discussion of principles of worship.
  - • *Worship Old and New* (Zondervan).
  - • *The Book of Family Prayer* (Thomas Nelson). A series of prayers that can be used on a variety of occasions.
- ◆ *Engaging with God: A Biblical Theology of Worship* by David Peterson (Eerdmans).
- ◆ *Worship His Majesty* by Jack W. Hayford (Word). A description of the charismatic (or praise) tradition of worship.
- ◆ *Worship in the Early Church* (Eerdmans) and *The Worship of God: Some Theological, Pastoral & Practical Reflections* (Eerdmans); by Ralph Martin.
- ◆ *The Book of Common Prayer* (Episcopal Church), 1979; *The Book of Services* (United Methodist Publishing House), 1985; *The Service for the Lord's Day* (Westminster), 1984. These are some of the services of worship used by various churches.

- *The New Westminster Dictionary of Liturgy and Worship* by J. G. Davies, ed. (Westminster/John Knox). If you are interested in a sympathetic description of each major tradition of Christian worship, consult this book.
- *I Believe in the Church* by David Watson (Eerdmans). A good survey of the nature and meaning of the church by an experienced pastor.
- *Christian Basics: A Handbook of Beginnings, Beliefs, and Behaviour* by John Stott (Baker). Chapter 9 is entitled "Fellowship and the Lord's Supper."
- *Word, Water, Wine & Bread: How Worship Has Changed over the Years* by William Willimon (Judson). The meaning of the sacraments in the context of worship.
- *Remember Who You Are: Baptism, a Model for Christian Life* by William Willimon (Upper Room).
- *Last Supper and Lord's Supper* by I. Howard Marshall (Paternoster).
- *Spiritual Traditions for the Contemporary Church* by Robin Maas and Gabriel O'Donnell (Abingdon). An excellent (though quite academic) survey of various ways of worship and spirituality.

Reflection Questions

1. A solitary Christian is a contradiction in terms. To become a Christian is to become a part of God's family. And God's family is not just a pious concept. It is a concrete reality. Week by week, all over the globe, groups of Christians meet to participate in the same activities as the first Christians. Reflect on your experience of the church:
   - Write down a history of your involvement with the church. Which churches have you attended? What impact (positive and negative) have they had on you? What did each experience mean to you?
   - What is the nature and extent of your participation now in the life of the church? What needs to change for you? What activities should you add? Drop?

2. Reflect on your baptism:
   - Baptism is, quite apart from anything else, the public declaration of your commitment to Jesus. In what ways was this your experience? How is your identification with the family of God expressed in your life?
   - If you were baptized as a child, what meaning does this have for you (even if you were an infant)? If you were baptized as an adult, what did the event mean to you? If you have yet to be baptized, when (and why) will you be baptized?
   - What does it mean to you to be "buried with Christ" and then to "rise to new life" with him?

3. Reflect on your experience of Communion:
   - When did you first take Communion? What did it mean to you?
   - What do you think about when you receive Communion?
   - What does Communion mean to you today?

---

[1] *Basic Christianity,* John Stott (Chicago: InterVarsity), pages 141–142.

Journal

Chapter Seven
Following God

Being a follower of God is a lifelong venture. Since we are in relationship with a Person (and not simply conforming to an ideology), we cannot know exactly how our path will unfold. The call to us as Christians is simply to walk faithfully in the ways of God.

We will explore the question of following God through a Bible study in which the group examines Abraham's pilgrimage as the model for the Christian's life (Hebrews 11:1–3,8–16); through an essay that discusses the process of pilgrimage; and by means of reflection on your own pilgrimage.

The hope is that in the small group experience and your own study, you will grow in your understanding of what it means to follow God.

Beginning (20 minutes)

When I grow up I wanna be...

Pilgrimage is not a new concept to us. We each are engaged in various pilgrimages: the one from child to adult; from single to married; from spouse to parent; from location to location. One important pilgrimage has to do with vocation: the path which led us to our present career.

1. When you were a child, how did you answer the question: "What do you want to be when you grow up?"

2. How were those dreams altered as you grew up? How did you arrive at your present vocation/occupation?

3. What dreams do you have about the future? What would you like to do (or to become) in the years ahead? How does this relate to your Christian pilgrimage?

The Text

The fundamental fact of existence is that this trust in God, **this faith**, is the firm foundation under everything that makes life worth living. It's our handle on what we can't see. The act of faith is what distinguished our ancestors, set them above the crowd. **By faith**, we see the world called into existence by God's word, what we see created by **what we don't see**....

By an act of faith, **Abraham said yes** to **God's call** to travel to **an unknown place** that would become his home. When he **left** he had **no idea where he was going**. By an act of faith he lived in the country promised him, lived as a stranger **camping in tents**. **Isaac and Jacob** did the same, living under the same promise. Abraham did it by **keeping his eye on an unseen city** with real, eternal foundations—the City designed and built by God.

By faith, **barren** Sarah was able to become pregnant, old woman as she was at the time, because she believed the One who made a promise would do what he said. That's how it happened that from one man's **dead and shriveled loins** there are now people numbering into the millions.

Each one of **these people of faith** died **not yet having in hand what was promised**, but still believing. How did they do it? They saw it way off in the distance, waved their greeting, and accepted the fact that they were **transients** in this world. People who live this way make it plain that they are looking for their true home. If they were homesick for **the old country**, they could have gone back any time they wanted. But they were after a far better country than that—*heaven* country. You can see why God is so proud of them, and has **a City waiting for them**.

Do you see what this means—all these **pioneers** who blazed the way, all these **veterans** cheering us on? It means we'd better get on with it. Strip down, start running—and **never quit**! No extra spiritual fat, no parasitic sins. **Keep your eyes on Jesus**, who both began and finished this **race** we're in. Study how he did it. Because he never lost sight of where he was headed—that exhilarating finish in and with God—he could put up with anything along the way: cross, shame, whatever. And now he's there, in the place of honor, right alongside God. When you find yourselves **flagging in your faith**, go over that story again, item by item, that long litany of hostility he plowed through. That will shoot adrenaline into your souls!

Hebrews 11:1–3;8–16;12:1–3
Eugene H. Peterson/The Message

Understanding the Text (20 minutes)

The idea of the Christian life as a pilgrimage to a heavenly city has roots deep in the Bible. Abraham was called by God to go out from his people into a new land. Moses left Egypt and led Israel to the promised land. Joshua took Israel into Canaan to make it their land. Jesus came down from heaven, walked the path of the cross, and led the way for all of us back to the Father in heaven. In this passage, the walk of faith is eloquently described.

1. Examine the text carefully by answering the following questions:
    ▶ What is faith, according to this passage?
    ▶ How is faith required to understand the creation of the universe?
    ▶ How do the lives of Abraham and Sarah illustrate what faith is?

2. Examine Abraham's journey:
   ▶ What was Abraham called to leave?
   ▶ What was he promised?
   ▶ What risk was he asked to take? What price did he pay?
   ▶ What hope lured him forward?

3. Examine the birth of Abraham and Sarah's son:
   ▶ Why was the idea of a son so preposterous?
   ▶ What was the result of this unlikely event?

4. What are the characteristics of those who live by faith?

5. What does all of this mean, according to Hebrews 12:1–3?
   ▶ What are we called upon to do and be?
   ▶ In what ways is Jesus our model?
   ▶ How are we encouraged and challenged by Hebrews 11–12?

Optional Exercise

Based on this passage, describe in your own words what the life of faith is.

Applying the Text (20 minutes)

1. Explore together the nature of faith:
   ▶ How does faith differ from wishful thinking?
   ▶ Is faith a concept, a feeling, an attitude, or an activity? Or all of these? Explain your response.
   ▶ How are faith and hope linked together?
   ▶ In what ways is faith involved in becoming a Christian?
   ▶ How is faith meant to function in our daily lives as Christians?
   ▶ What does it mean for you, right now, to live by faith?

2. Now explore what it means to live as pilgrims in this world:
   ▶ Where are we called to go? Why?
   ▶ What resources sustain us on this lifelong journey?
   ▶ What difference does it make that we are not called to be solitary pilgrims, but to be part of a band of joyous pilgrims (the church)?

3. In what ways is Abraham's pilgrimage the model for our pilgrimage? What aspect of his pilgrimage resonates most strongly with your own experience?

4. In what ways does the realization that we will one day dwell with God affect how we live today?

5. Where do you sense you are in your spiritual pilgrimage? Where would you like to be next year? Five years from now? Twenty years from now?

Optional Exercise

The life of pilgrimage contains various events that shape it. Identify the key events in the unfolding of your spiritual life. Events might include such things as a conversion experience, a painful experience that challenged your faith, an affirming event that convinced you that you were on the right road, a prayer experience, a ministry experience. Share these with the group.

Bible Study Notes

Setting: Hebrews 11 is a celebration of faith, expressed through the stories of saints of old. We look at one story in this catalog of faith, that of Abraham. The journey of Abraham to the land of Canaan was a powerful metaphor for the people of Israel. It became the image of what God called them to as a nation: obedient pilgrimage to the promised land (e.g., Palestine, the eventual home of the Jewish people; the New Jerusalem, the heavenly home of all God's people).

this faith: The life of faith is based on a deep belief and trust in God and in his promises.

By faith: An example of faith is our conviction, though we could never know it directly, that God created the physical world by his word of command.

what we don't see: The literal translation is: "faith is…the conviction of things not seen."

Abraham: Abraham is considered the "father of all who believe" (Romans 4:11); the model of what a life of faith is all about. The story of Abraham is told in Genesis 11:27–25:11.

said yes: Faith produces action. God called; Abraham obeyed.

God's call: God called Abraham to leave his country and travel to a place where he would make Abraham a great nation (see Genesis 12:1–9).

an unknown place: This was Canaan, the promised land, which would become Palestine.

left: Abraham lived in what was then the center of the civilized world. Ur of the Chaldeans (probably in southern Iraq) had a high level of culture.

no idea where he was going: What Abraham was promised was nowhere in sight.

camping in tents: Abraham was a nomad, not staying long in any place.

Isaac and Jacob: Abraham's son and grandson, through whom the nation of Israel would emerge.

keeping his eye on an unseen city: Abraham's strong sense that God had prepared a place for him made it possible to undertake this journey of faith. Faith and hope work together: faith is the attitude of trust that keeps us going; hope is the confidence that what we have believed is real and not just wishful thinking.

barren…dead and shriveled loins: Sarah was beyond the years of childbearing (Genesis 18:11), and Abraham was 100 years old when his son was born (well past the age when he could father a child).

these people of faith: In verses 4–7, the author recounts the faith of Abel, Enoch, and Noah.

not yet having in hand what was promised: These OT figures did not experience in their lifetimes the heavenly realities that they knew one day would be theirs.

transients: This is the usual status for followers of Jesus: men and women passing through this life on the way to the heavenly city which is our true home. We are pilgrims.

the old country: Where we "lived" before we met Christ; the old life of sin and disintegration.

a City waiting for them: In the final sense, this is the New Jerusalem (described in Revelation 21). This is the ultimate dwelling place of the family of God. It is dominated by the presence of God, and is characterized by his perfection.

pioneers/veterans: Other names for pilgrims. The literal rending is "host of witnesses."

never quit!: This is the response that the writer is seeking from us—endurance: hanging in there when things get tough for us as people of faith.

Keep your eyes on Jesus: Jesus is our model; he is our example. We see in him the twin attributes of faithfulness and endurance that the writer of Hebrews urges us to emulate. His death on the cross is "the supreme example of persevering faith" (Lane).

race: The metaphor of an athletic contest is used.

flagging in your faith: This is one of the central issues that concerns the writer of Hebrews. He has written to encourage those who are struggling (due largely to outside pressure put on them by a culture that was hostile to Christianity).

Comment

Pilgrimage

Loving God is different from loving doctrine. Doctrine (true ideas about God and his ways) is important. It is crucial that our minds are as soundly converted as our hearts. But in the end, ideas are just ideas; whereas God is alive—a flame of love, a presence, a power, a reality, a person. Ideas can be embraced, but God can be loved. Once ideas are accepted and one's life is conformed to them, the matter is over. But when God becomes the center of life, the story has just begun. How it will unfold, where you will be led, who will play a part in your life, what task you will be asked to undertake, where you will go—all of that will emerge in the context of your relationship with God.

Relationships are like that: they unfold over time. The people of Israel had no idea where God was leading them. They knew what the end would be: they would live in a land flowing with milk and honey. But how they would get there, what lay ahead for them, how they would react to changing circumstances, how faithful to God they would be—well, they had to live out the story in relationship to God.

The same is true for us. We know the end of the story: we will dwell in the New Jerusalem, where death is undone and tears no longer exist. We will abide in the presence of God. Heaven is our heritage. This fact informs our whole lives as it unfolds. We know heaven to be our goal.

And we also know that we have a journey ahead of us. The way will be long. We will not always follow well. We will be accompanied by many other joyful pilgrims. We will have tasks to do (as we play our part in the Kingdom of God). We will need to learn how to love God, love ourselves, and love others.

The Christian life is no static holding action; it is an amazing, serendipitous journey. To live it out is our calling in life. As we do so, we become what we are meant to be: whole people, holy people, conformed to the image of Christ. This is our great and wonderful task in life.

This, then, is the sum of it:

- ◆ Our goal is heaven.
- ◆ Our path is faithfulness.
- ◆ Our life is pilgrimage.

May God grant each of us grace to be what God calls us to be.

The Art of Bible Study

The Process of Observation

It is important to remember why the observation process is undertaken in the first place: to cause us, the readers, to notice what is there in the passage. Unless we notice the details of the text, we cannot interpret the passage properly. A number of observation techniques have been discussed in the first six chapters. If you followed all of these suggestions for each passage, you would have no time left to interpret (much less apply) what is being said! The important thing is to use the observation methodology that is appropriate for each passage.

If you go back over the Bible studies in this book, you will see that only certain observation exercises are undertaken. In preparing these observation exercises, the question was asked: What will help the reader notice what is going on in this particular passage? Fit your observation to the particular passage you are studying.

There are other approaches to observation that you can use besides the basic ones which have already been discussed:

❏ **Important Words:** Go through the passage and circle each word that is important. Important words tend to be those words that are:
  ▶ *Repeated:* repetition is often a sign that the word is significant to the author.
  ▶ *Parallel:* watch for words that have similar meaning. This is a form of repetition.
  ▶ *Unusual:* if the author hasn't used the word before, you probably need to pay attention to it.
  ▶ *Loaded:* certain words are stuffed with a lot of content (e.g., gospel, kingdom, repent), and they need to be "unpacked" (i.e., carefully defined so that we may grasp their full meaning).

❏ **Functional Words:** go through the passage and find the words that define the structure of the passage:
  ▶ *Circle* the main nouns that define the setting.
  ▶ Put a *square* around the verbs that define the action.
  ▶ *Underline* the important clauses or phrases.
  ▶ *Connect* words that belong together with lines.
  ▶ *Color* code similar words.

❏ **Noticing:** Go through the passage and "notice" as much as you can. What catches your eye? What strikes you as unusual? What puzzles you? What is familiar? What is new? See how many observations you can make. Then go back over your observations and identify the really significant ones.

❏ **Questioning:** Read through a passage and start writing down questions that occur to you. Some questions will be answered by the passage itself; others will need further investigation. Asking the right questions is half the battle in making sense out of a passage. See how many questions you can write for each passage.

Exercise: Go through the Hebrews passage and try one of these observation techniques. What new facts or insights do you discover in the passage?

Extra Reading

- *Pilgrimage* by Richard Peace (Baker). An examination of the pilgrim lifestyle, including a series of exercises to encourage your own pilgrimage.
- *Following the Master: Discipleship in the Steps of Jesus* by Michael J. Wilkins (Zondervan). A study that seeks to clarify from a biblical and historical point of view what discipleship is meant to be.
- *The Cost of Discipleship* by Dietrich Bonhoeffer (Macmillan). A classic exposition of the Sermon on the Mount by a Lutheran pastor who was killed by Hitler during World War II for his opposition to Nazism. Bonhoeffer contrasts cheap grace with costly (real) grace.
- *The Spirit of the Disciplines: Understanding How God Changes Lives* by Dallas Willard (Harper & Row). Willard argues that undertaking spiritual disciplines is not a sign of exceptional spirituality, but the evidence of a desire to learn how to live as Christ intends. The disciplines help us to do what is not natural for us.
- *A Quest for Godliness: The Puritan Vision of the Christian Life* by J. I. Packer (Crossway). Puritans are often caricatured as pharisaical, joyless law-keepers. In fact, as Packer shows, they had a spirituality which was lively and vigorous.
- *Christian Spirituality: Five Views of Sanctification* by Donald Alexander, ed. (InterVarsity). A discussion among five scholars about the doctrine of sanctification. Sanctification is the theological term for growth in the Christian graces.
- *Invitation to Pilgrimage* by John Baillie (Pelican). An insightful and personal analysis of Christian belief and the Christian way of life by an eminent Scottish theologian.
- *Life on the Road: The Gospel Basis for a Messianic Lifestyle* by Athol Gill (Australia: Lancer Books). A biblical scholar from Australia explores the Gospels for clues about our lifestyle. A challenging book that calls us to a deep and costly discipleship.
- *Invitation to Discipleship* by Myron S. Augsburger (Herald).
- *Taking Discipleship Seriously: A Radical Biblical Approach* by Tom Sine (Judson).
- *Called and Committed: World Changing Discipleship* by David Watson (Harold Shaw).

Reflection Questions

Examine carefully the nature of your own spiritual pilgrimage:

▶ Return to the key events you identified in the *Optional Exercise* in the *Applying the Text* section (page 65). Reflect on these events. In what ways were they important to you? How did they shape who you are now? Who you are becoming?

▶ Look at your life as a whole. Each person's life is characterized by various phases. Quite often the phases of our lives are determined by our educational experience: preschool, elementary school, middle school, high school, college—each of these time periods has a different shape to it. Other realities also shape the phases of our lives: the influence of an important person for a period of time, living in a particular place, marriage, a creative project, work assignments. Identify the various phases of your life up to this point in time. Then put these on a graph. Make the bottom line (horizontal axis) a time line from birth to your present age. Then divide the time line into your various phases. For each period of time, reflect on the level of your spiritual awareness. Let the vertical portion of your graph represent the "Level of spiritual awareness." Then plot your spiritual pilgrimage over time, through the different phases of your life.

▶ Reflect on how each phase shaped your spiritual awareness.

▶ Reflect on your career pilgrimage. In what ways can (and do) you serve God in your vocation? Is God calling you to a new vocation?

▶ Commit your pilgrimage to God in prayer. Ask God to continue to guide and direct you. Be sensitive to where God is leading you in the future. Are there important decisions you need to make about your unfolding pilgrimage?

Journal

The Art of Leadership
Brief Reflections on How to Lead a Small Group

It is not difficult to be a small group leader. All you need is:

- ◆ the willingness to do so.
- ◆ the commitment to read through all the materials prior to the session (including the leader's notes for that session).
- ◆ the sensitivity to others that will allow you to guide the discussion without dominating it.
- ◆ the willingness to have God use you as a small group leader.

Here are some basic small group principles that will help you to do your job.

Ask the questions: Your role is to ask the group to respond to each of the questions in the study guide. Simply read the questions and let various group members respond.

Guide the discussion: Ask follow-up questions (or make comments) that draw others into the discussion, and keep the discussion going. For example:

- ◆ "John, how would you answer the question?"
- ◆ "Anybody else have any insights into this question?"
- ◆ "Let's move on to the next question."

Start and stop on time: Your job is to start the group on time and (most importantly) to stop it on time. Certain people will always be late, so don't wait until they arrive. Make sure you end on time. If you don't, people will be hesitant to come again since they never know when they will get home.

Stick to the time allotted to each section: There is always more that can be said in response to any question. So if you do not stick very carefully to the time limits for each section, you will never finish the study. And this usually means the group will miss out on the very important application questions at the end of the session. It is your job to make sure that the discussion keeps moving from question to question. You may have to keep saying: "Well, it is time to move on to the next question." Remember: it is better to cut off discussion when it is going well than to let it go on until it dies out.

Model answers to questions: Whenever you ask a question to which everyone is expected to respond (for example, a *Beginning* question as opposed to a Bible study question), you, as leader, should be the first person to answer. In this way, you show others the right amount of time to respond. If you take 5 minutes to respond, everyone else in the group will feel that it is okay for them to take at least 5 minutes (so one question will take 50 minutes for the whole group to answer!). But if you take one minute to answer, so will everyone else (and the question takes only 10 minutes for the group to answer). Also, by responding first, you model an appropriate level of openness. Remember, the leader should be just a little bit more open than others.

Understand the intention of different kinds of questions: You will ask the group various kinds of questions. It is important for you to understand the purpose of each kind of question:

◆ *Experience questions:* These are often the first type of questions you will ask. The aim of these questions is to cause people to recall past experiences and share these memories with the group. There is no right or wrong answer to these questions. Such questions facilitate the group process by:
  • getting people to share their stories with one another.
  • being easy to answer, so everyone has something to say and thus the group conversation begins.
  • getting people to think about the session topic on the basis of their own experience.

◆ *Forced-choice questions:* Certain questions will be followed by a series of suggested answers (with check-boxes next to each possible answer). Generally, no particular answer is correct. In fact, often each answer is correct. By offering options, group members are aided in responding. This also helps direct the response. When people answer such questions, you may want to ask them to explain why they chose the answer they did.

◆ *Analysis questions:* These are questions that force the group to notice what the biblical text says and to probe it for meaning.

◆ *Application questions:* These questions help the group make connections between the meaning of the text and each person's life circumstance.

◆ *Questions with multiple parts:* Sometimes a question is asked and then various aspects of it are listed below. Have the group answer each of the sub-questions. Their answers, taken together, will answer the initial question.

Introduce each section: It is your job to introduce each section. This may involve:

◆ *Overview:* Briefly explain the focus, purpose, and/or topic of the new section.

◆ *Instructions:* Explain how to do the exercise.

Comments: Occasionally it will be helpful to the group if you bring into the discussion some useful information that you have discovered from your own study. Never make long comments. Do not allow yourself to become the "expert" whom everyone turns to for "the right answer." Invite comments from others.

Some comments about how the small group discussion is structured in this book:

There are four parts to each small group session, and each has a different aim:

◆ *Beginning:* The purpose of this section is to:
  • Help people to move from the worries and concerns they brought with them (to the group) to the topic itself.
  • Start people thinking about the topic in terms of their own experiences.
  • Start discussion among group members.
  • Encourage people to tell their stories to each other so they get to know one another.

◆ *Reading the Text:* The purpose of this section is to:
  • Start the process of analyzing the text.
  • Let people hear what they will then study. Reading helps people to notice things in the text they might not see otherwise.
  • Focus on the text as the core of the small group study.

- *Understanding the Text:* The purpose of this section is to:
  - Immerse people in the text, so that they start to see what is there (the observation process).
  - Discern the main points of the text.
  - Understand the text as first-century hearers might have understood it.
- *Applying the Text:* The purpose of this section is to:
  - Understand what the text is saying (the interpretation process).
  - Apply the text to people's lives (the application process).

Begin each new session by:
- *Welcoming everyone.*
- *Opening in prayer:* Your prayer does not need to be long or complex. You can write it out beforehand. In your prayer, thank God for his presence. Ask him to guide the group into new wisdom, and to give each person the courage to respond to the text. You do not have to be the one who always opens in prayer. You can ask others to pray. It is usually a good idea to ask beforehand if a person is willing to pray aloud.
- *Introducing the topic:* Take no more than one minute to do this. Simply identify what you will be discussing, the text you will be studying, and the main ideas you will be examining. You will find this introductory material on the first page of each chapter.

Move to the *Beginning* exercise:
- Read the brief introduction aloud (when there is one), or just introduce the theme of the exercise.
- Give people a minute to read over the questions and think about their answers.
- Then as leader, begin the sharing by giving your answer to the first question:
  - Remember, there are no "right" answers—only personal stories or preferences.
  - Laughter is great medicine. These questions are seldom serious and invite funny stories (often from childhood).
- Move to the person on your right and ask him or her to respond.
- Go around the circle, so each person has a chance to respond to the question.
- Move to question two and do the same thing.
- Finish up with question three.
- Watch the time carefully so everyone has a chance to respond:
  - Don't worry if you do not get through all three questions, as long as people have started sharing.
  - After a few sessions, you will know how many questions you can get through with your group. You may need to pre-select one or two questions to use for this sharing time.
- Remember that even though this is lighthearted sharing, you are discussing the topic of the Bible study. Remind people of the theme of the subject.

Move to the second section of the small group study—*Understanding the Text:*
- Introduce the Bible passage by reading aloud (or summarizing in your own words) the introduction to this section.
- Read the Bible passage (or invite someone else to read it).
- Give the group a few minutes to read over the passage, read through the questions (and think about the answers), and to consult the *Bible Study Notes.*

- Ask question one:
  - Get responses from several people.
- When you feel that the question has been sufficiently discussed, move to the next question.
  - In this section, some of the initial questions are fact-oriented. There are specific answers to them. Subsequent questions will be more open-ended and will invite discussion.
- Work through all of the questions:
  - Be sure you have worked through the questions yourself beforehand, so that you know which are the important questions that need more time.
- If you still have time left for this section, use the optional question (where there is one). These invite a lot of discussion and personal sharing that will fill the remaining time.
  - You may decide to skip some questions and end with the *Optional Question* or *Exercise.*
- Remember: your aim in this section is to help the group notice what the text says and to begin to interpret it.

Move to the final section of the small group study—*Applying the Text:*
- Follow the same discussion process as the *Understanding the Text* section.
- Remember: your aim in this section is to help the group grasp the meaning of the text and to apply it to their lives.

Conclude the small group session:
- Discuss the *Personal Study* section for the coming week:
  - Encourage people to read over the *Bible Study Notes* (if they have not had time to do so during the small group).
  - Encourage the group to read the *Comment* section.
  - Encourage people to study and then work on the ideas in *The Art of Bible Study* section.
  - Encourage people to do *Journal* work.
- End with prayer together.

Serve coffee, tea, soft drinks, etc.:
- This will give people a chance to talk informally.
- There is often very good conversation following a small group session, as people hash over the evening's discussion.

Additional Exercises: There are a number of ways to enrich your small group session. You may want to add an extra exercise each week (e.g., start off each session with *Journal* sharing). Or you can vary the nature of the extra exercise (e.g., one week do a case study; the next week do a book report, etc.). What follows are suggestions for alternative or additional small group exercises.

Sub-Groups: You may want to divide the group into sub-groups of four for part of the sharing. This allows more time for each person to participate. Also, people who might be intimidated in a group of twelve find it easier to talk in a group of four.

♦ It is best to begin and end the session with everyone together.

♦ Do not form permanent sub-groups. Each week, have a different foursome meet together in a sub-group. In this way you maintain the identity of the whole group.

Journal: You may want to set aside time each week for people to share from their *Journals.* This can be a very powerful experience—you will discuss on a deep level the personal meaning of the previous week's passage.

♦ It is probably best to do this at the beginning of the session before you get into the new material.

Book Report: Bring along one (or more) of the books in the *Extra Reading* section:

♦ Discuss the content of the book.

♦ Ask someone else to discuss one of the books.

Comment: You may want to focus on the *Comment* section.

♦ Give people time to read it over (or read it aloud).

♦ Prepare questions that will enable the group to discuss the ideas in the *Comment* section.

Bible Study Notes: Some weeks you may want to spend time on these notes as a way of deepening the understanding of the text.

♦ You can do this by allowing more time for individual study of the text. Group members can then think about how they would answer each study question in light of the information in the notes.

The Art of Bible Study: It will be helpful to go over the process of Bible study from time to time—to encourage people to read and analyze the Bible on their own.

♦ Have someone report to the group about their experience in using some of these techniques.

♦ Make comments occasionally about *how* the group is analyzing the text at that moment. By doing this, you will highlight certain Bible study principles.

Sharing: Each week, ask a different person in the group to take five minutes and share how he or she came to faith. Or ask people to share how they applied biblical insights (from the previous study) to their lives during the week.

Case study: Tell the actual story of somebody you know (or read about) and then ask the group: How can the principles we have studied in this text help in this situation?

Small Group Leader's Guide
Notes on Each Session

If you are the small group leader, it is important for you to read carefully the section entitled *The Art of Leadership: Brief Reflections on How to Lead the Small Group.* This will help you in the art of small group leadership. It will also give you ideas on how you can tailor the material to fit the needs of your specific group. Then prior to each session, go over the notes for that session (see below). These will focus on the specific materials in the session.

Chapter One: Encountering God

1

The special character of Session One: The first session is most important. During this session, those who attend will be deciding whether they want to be a part of the group. So your aim as small group leader is to:
- ► Create excitement about being part of this particular small group (so that each person will want to continue in the group).
- ► Give people an overview of the whole series (so they will know where the group is headed).
- ► Begin to build relationships (so that a sense of community starts to develop).
- ► Encourage commitment to be a part of the small group (so that everyone will return next week, and bring along a friend!).

Pot Luck: A good way to launch the first session of any small group is by eating together prior to the session. Sharing a meal draws people together and breaks down barriers between them.
- ► Ask everyone to bring one dish for the supper. This makes it easy to have a meal for twelve! Or if you feel ambitious, you might want to invite everyone to dinner at your place. What you serve doesn't need to be elaborate. Conversation (not feasting) is the intention of the get-together.
- ► The aim of the meal is to get to know one another in this informal setting. Structure the meal in such a way that a lot of conversation takes place.
- ► Following the meal, be sure to complete the first Bible study (and not just talk about what you are going to do when the group starts). Your aim is to give everyone the experience of what it would mean to be a part of this small group.

Introduction to the Bible Study
- ► *Welcome:* Greet the small group and let them know how glad you are that they have come, and how much you look forward to being with them for the next seven weeks.
- ► *Prayer:* Pray briefly—thank God for bringing this group together, and ask him to guide your deliberations and sharing today (and in the weeks ahead). Ask God to touch each life in such a way as to meet the deep needs of that person.
- ► *Group Process:* Describe how the small group will function and what it will study. Discuss specifically:

- *Series Theme:* In the seven small group sessions, you will be discussing what it means to love God. Read the titles of each session to the group to illustrate how this theme will be developed.
- *Group Process:* Describe how each session will be conducted. Explain that each session will begin with a brief time of sharing (in which the topic is introduced by means of experiences group members have had). Then you will study a passage from the Bible together, using the questions in this study guide. These questions will help you come to grips with what the passage means and how it applies to your lives.
- *Group Details:* Describe where you will meet, when, and how long each session will last.
- *Group Aims:* The hope is that group members will grow in their understanding of what it means to know and love God; that they will apply these insights to their lives; and that they will begin to understand how to study the Bible on their own. Share these aims with the group.

Beginning
- ▶ Give the group a minute to look over the questions and decide on answers.
- ▶ Begin the small group sharing. As leader, you should be the first one to answer each question. Go around the group and give each person a chance to respond to the first question. Do the same for each question until time is up for the exercise.
- ▶ *Question 1:* Listen carefully to the various reasons that drew people to the group. This is the implicit agenda for the group. These are the needs, hopes, and issues that the group needs to deal with.
- ▶ *Question 2:* The issue here is how we acquire accurate information about God.
- ▶ *Question 3:* This question gets at the issue of motivation: what has drawn us into the search to know God?

Understanding the Text
- ▶ *The Text:* There are various ways of presenting the passage. It is probably best to have someone read it aloud. Ask for a volunteer, or read it aloud yourself. (Never ask a person to read aloud without first getting their permission. Some adults have trouble reading aloud.) Then give the group a few minutes to go over the passage on their own, examining the questions and the *Bible Study Notes.*
- ▶ *Question 1:* This question has five parts. Use it to get discussion started as group members quickly identify the facts about Paul in the passage. Do not spend a lot of time on this observation question.
- ▶ *Question 2:* This is another multiple-answer observation question. Use it to develop an understanding of Paul's mystical encounter with Jesus.
- ▶ *Question 4:* This is a more speculative question (in that it moves away from the description in the passage to the very human feelings of both Ananias and Paul).
- ▶ *Optional Questions:* If you still have time left before moving to *Applying the Text,* ask these questions. You may want to assign them as homework questions, to be answered during the *Journal* reflections. The first question asks the group to reflect on Paul's experience as an example of

a mystical experience. The second is a reflection on how someone like Paul could come to know Christ.

Applying the Text

▶ *Question 1:* This is a synthesis question (in which the group is asked to create a portrait of Paul based on this passage).

▶ *Question 2:* This question moves the group from the passage to the personal experiences of group members.

▶ *Question 3:* It may be that not every group member has come to faith. Thus this question is phrased so that anyone can answer it.

▶ *Questions 4 and 5:* These questions ask the group to apply their understanding of the text to themselves.

▶ *Optional Questions:* It will be useful for group members to share stories about meeting God. It will also be instructive to discuss connections between their stories and the stories of the five people in the *Comment* section.

Concluding Issues

▶ *Group Covenant:* Have the group turn to the section entitled: *How to Use It: Questions About the Study Guide.* Give the group a few minutes to look over the *Group Covenant* (page 14). Make sure everyone is comfortable with these ground rules. Conclude by going around the group and asking each member to agree to the covenant.

▶ *Group Invitation:* If your first session is a "trial meeting," invite all who attended to return next week for chapter 2. Returning for the second week will usually mean that they are committed for the duration of the series (six more weeks). If you have room in the small group (i.e., there are less than twelve people), encourage group members to invite friends for the second session. After week two, no new members can join the group (since each time a new person comes it is necessary to rebuild the sense of community).

▶ *Group Homework:* Some leaders may ask members to prepare certain materials for the next session. If you decide to do this, go over the homework at this point. You might want to ask people to work through the *Comment* section and put their observations in their *Journals.* Or perhaps you can ask each person to be prepared the following week to share a brief *Journal* entry.

▶ *Group Prayer:* End with a time of prayer. Pray in a way that is comfortable for your group (i.e., you may lead in prayer, ask someone to pray, let various people pray briefly as led by God, etc., depending upon the group).

Other Materials

▶ Since this is the first session, it will probably be useful to the group for you to go over the *Study Resources* and *Personal Study* sections of the book, so everyone knows how these fit into the whole course.

• *Bible Study Notes:* Sometimes there is not enough time during the small group to do little more than glance at these notes. In this case, it would be helpful for people to read them carefully on their own as a way of deepening their understanding of the text.

• *Comment:* You may choose not to use the *Comment* section, so it can be studied during the week by each individual.

• *The Art of Bible Study:* A person who reads this carefully will (over the course of the twenty-one sessions in the three books) learn the fundamentals of the inductive Bible study process. The hope is that these insights will enable such a person to study the Bible more profitably on his or her own.

- *Extra Reading:* Point out the variety of books that will allow further research on issues of interest.
- *Reflection Questions:* These will guide personal reflection in the *Journal* section.

▶ You may want to use some of this material as homework which would then be discussed in the next session.

Chapter Two: Knowing God

2

Introduction

▶ *Welcome:* Greet the group and let them know how glad you are that they are all there. This means they have decided to be part of the group for the next six weeks. Tell them how much you are looking forward to your time together.

▶ *Prayer:* Pray briefly, thanking God for what he is doing in each person's life and asking him to guide your deliberations and sharing today. Pray that during this session God will make it crystal clear to each person how to know him.

▶ *Theme:* Refer people to the introduction to chapter 2 and the issue that will be discussed today.

Beginning

▶ *Question 1:* This probes childhood images of God. Remember that not everyone will have a clear memory. But encourage people to recall how they thought about God when they were children.

▶ *Question 2:* It is one thing to have an image of God; it is another to respond to this God. Depending upon their circumstances, different people will feel differently about the God they knew as children.

Understanding the Text

▶ *The Text:* Have someone read the text aloud. Then give the group a few minutes to go over the passage on their own, examining the questions and the *Bible Study Notes.*

▶ *Question 1:* There are a variety of people in this passage. This question will help you to get the "cast of characters" straight. Spend only a minute on this "fact" question.

▶ *Question 2:* This question helps the group to see clearly the nature of the event that precipitates this episode.

▶ *Questions 3–6:* These questions probe the reaction to the earthquake and results of this event.

▶ *Optional Question:* Try to leave enough time to answer this question. This will be the first attempt on the part of the group to identify personal connections with what happened in the passage. If you don't discuss this question as a group, you may want to assign it as a homework question (to be answered during the *Journal* reflections).

Applying the Text

▶ *Questions 1 and 2:* These questions probe the various reactions to this event.

▶ *Question 3:* Before a person can (or will) come to know God, there has to be some reason to do so. Often we turn to God out of a sense of deep need. This question looks at the issue of need and how it opens us up to God.

▶ *Question 4:* This is a key question in this study. It looks at how people come to know God and examines the key words in the process. You will want to refer to the information in the *Bible Study Notes* and in the *Comment* section as the group answers this question. You may want to give the group a few minutes to read this material as they prepare to answer question 4.

▶ *Optional Question:* These questions also refer to the *Comment* section as they clarify what is involved in coming to know God.

Concluding Issues

▶ Assign homework (if any) and conclude in prayer together. Pray that each person will be clear about his or her relationship with God.

Other Materials

▶ You may want to use other sections from this chapter as part of your small group session.

▶ *Comment:* You may have used some of this material already in your discussion. These essays are so important in clarifying how to know God that you may want to discuss the material in even more detail. The questions in the *Journal* section may help you to do this.

▶ *Extra Reading:* These books (and booklets) will help people with questions to follow them up. You may want to bring some of the books to the small group and loan them to interested members. You could purchase copies of one or more of the (inexpensive) booklets and give them out to group members. These include: *Becoming a Christian, Have You Considered Him?* or *Why I Believe in Christ.*

▶ *The Art of Bible Study:* If your group will be learning how to do Bible study, set aside some time to discuss the ideas in this section.

Chapter Three: Being Sure We Know God

3

Introduction

▶ *Prayer:* Pray briefly—thank God for what he is doing in each person's life, and ask God to guide your deliberations and sharing today. Pray that during this session, God will make it crystal clear to each person how we come to know him.

▶ *Theme:* Refer people to the introduction to Chapter Three and the issue that will be discussed today.

Beginning

▶ Since the theme of the study is assurance, this exercise helps people in their awareness of the presence of God.

▶ *Question 1:* This question asks people to recall how they first became aware of God.

▶ *Question 2:* This moves people from the past to the present. Awareness of

God is not something that happens only once (e.g., at conversion), but often. Awareness of God isn't always dramatic; more often, it's a small and simple awareness that comes in a variety of ways.

Understanding the Text
- ▶ This week you get to examine two texts! What this means is that you must watch the time carefully. Either text could be the sole focus of the Bible study (since both are so rich in meaning). However, it is important (given the theme of the session—assurance of salvation) to cover both passages. They each deal with a different and important aspect of the subject. Be sure to keep your focus in this discussion. The passage from John describes how a person comes to Christ (and thus assures us that we have done so). The passage in Romans shows that we are eternally secure in Christ (and so assures us that we will not lose our salvation).
- ▶ *Question 1:* Go through these questions quickly. They are designed to ensure that the group has noticed all the elements in the passage from John.
- ▶ *Question 2:* These are more significant questions, in that they get at the meaning of the passage.
  - Part One: Here you are asking the group to remember some of the details of Jesus' birth in Bethlehem. Everyone knows the Christmas story, so this should result in good sharing.
  - Part Two: To get at this question, you might want to ask: "What do you think it might feel like for you to become an ant and live in an anthill?"
  - Part Four: Notice the role of belief, and recall the definition of "believing" in chapter 2.
- ▶ *Question 3:*
  - Part One: You might want to write each answer on a chalkboard as they are called out by the group. Or have people number each of the "enemies" in their books.
  - Part Two: This will uncover the nature of the peril in each instance. For example, the allure of the world ("life") may appear so strong that it could move a person away from faith. Don't worry about going over each of the seventeen. Just look at a few and the reasons why Paul might have listed them as potential enemies that could wrest us from the love of God. Help the group to see that the love of God is present and powerful in each circumstance.
- ▶ *Optional Question:* Here you might want to consider such fears as: the fear that some people have that they are not worthy of Christ; the fear that they will commit an unpardonable sin; the fear that they are believing fables. In each case, the fear can be defused by seeing what the Bible has to say about it. This is how the two fears in this chapter are dealt with.
  - Thus, we find that the fear we are not worthy is meaningless (since we don't come to Christ on the basis of who we are or what we have or have not done). We come solely on the basis of what Christ has done for us (see Ephesians 2:1–10).
  - The so-called unpardonable sin is simply the refusal to ask for forgiveness. We cannot receive forgiveness if we do not ask (see Mark 3:20–30, noting especially verse 28).
  - As for the question of the historicity (truth) of Christ, this can be dealt with in many ways. One way is to examine the resurrection accounts

carefully. It will become clear that the most logical explanation of the empty tomb is that Jesus rose from the dead. And if he rose from the dead, he is who he claimed to be (and he is still alive today, so that we can be in relationship with him). The challenge in discussing this question is that it requires a good biblical background on the part of the leader, so that he or she can find texts that address each issue.

Applying the Text

▶ *Questions 1 and 2:* These two questions deal with how we come to know who Jesus is. They may (or may not) be important questions for your group. Include (or drop) them from the discussion, depending upon your group.

▶ *Question 4:* This is an important question, since it helps people to see that the issue of whether or not we are a Christian is not decided by how we feel. Feelings come and go, but the fact remains that when we accept Christ, we are a Christian, no matter how we feel.

▶ *Question 5:* What this question addresses is the kind of threat which would have the biggest impact on us (as far as our security as children of God is concerned).

▶ *Question 6:* You could paraphrase this by asking: "How has the love of Christ enabled you to cope in difficult times?"

▶ *Question 7:* This is the key question in this study. You should give each person a chance to respond. Perhaps you should respond first. If people have understood the lesson, they will know that when a person reaches out in faith to Jesus, then that person is a Christian. This is the assurance Scripture gives us. Our feelings do not matter. We must trust what the Bible says. Group members will also understand that there is nothing that can separate them from the love of God. This assurance will enable them to grow in their Christian lives.

▶ *Optional Questions:* These two questions focus on the two issues of this chapter: not feeling saved, and fearing that we might lose our salvation.

Concluding Issues

▶ Assign homework (if any) and conclude in prayer together. Pray that each person will be clear about his or her relationship with God.

Chapter Four: Learning About God

Introduction

▶ *Prayer:* Pray briefly—thank God for what he is doing in each person's life, and ask God to guide your deliberations and sharing today. Pray that during this session, you will develop a new love of (and interest in) Scripture.

▶ *Theme:* Refer people to the introduction to chapter 4 and the issue that will be discussed today.

Beginning

▶ Kids receive various kinds of religious training. The exercise today helps people to remember what did or did not happen in their early religious education, and how they feel about it now.

- ▶ *Question 1:* Be sensitive to the fact that not everyone had formal religious education as a child.
- ▶ *Question 2:* Different people respond in different ways to Sunday school. And those who did not have formal religious education may have had an informal teacher (a friend, relative, television, books they read, etc.)—an issue which one of the choices recognizes.
- ▶ *Question 3:* This will generate good discussion. How can we teach children about God so that it will be a positive experience, and that they will come to love God?

Understanding the Text

- ▶ *Question 1:* Go through these questions quickly. They are designed to help the group notice all the elements of the passage.
- ▶ *Question 4:* If you have time, ask someone to read this passage aloud.
- ▶ *Question 5:* As with other observation questions, linger on this one.
- ▶ *Optional Questions:* These questions will help people recall their contact with the Bible as children and as adults—what it was and what it meant to them.

Applying the Text

- ▶ *Question 1:* Different people have different levels of Bible knowledge. It's important to acknowledge what we know (and do not know) about the Bible. Our aim is to grow in our knowledge of Scripture.
- ▶ *Question 2:* It's important to establish the habit of regular Bible study.
- ▶ *Question 4:* This will give group members a chance to share how they have been changed by the Bible.
- ▶ *Optional Questions:* The first question helps each group member to set goals for him or herself. The second generates conversation about the nature of inspiration.

Concluding Issues

- ▶ Assign homework (if any) and conclude in prayer together. Pray that the Bible will become a life-changing light for each person in the group.

Chapter Five: Conversing with God

5

Beginning

- ▶ *Question 1:* A lot of children are taught simple prayers. Although these are often more ritual than anything, at least it reminds children that God exists and can hear prayer.
- ▶ *Question 2:* Prayer (if not belief) becomes a lot more serious for a teenager. Usually these prayers are of the "Lord, don't let my parents find out what I did" kind.
- ▶ *Question 3:* Of course, the real issue is how we respond to prayer as adults. This question begins to address this issue.

Understanding the Text

▶ *Question 1:* In this section of the Sermon on the Mount, Jesus discusses the right and the wrong way to go about certain religious observances. This question helps the group to see the kind of prayer to avoid.

▶ *Question 2:* The *Bible Study Notes* will help you to identify the six requests.

▶ *Question 3:* This question is the heart of the discussion: making sure each phrase in the prayer is understood.

▶ *Optional Question:* This addresses our assumptions about prayer.

Applying the Text

▶ *Question 1:* This concerns our motivation to pray, both positive and negative.

▶ *Question 2:* This is one of the questions we often ask about prayer. There is no single answer to this question, only a number of different approaches. In the end it is a mystery. God invites us to prayer, even when he knows the end from the beginning. And God uses our prayers. Our prayers are part of his plan. You should have an excellent discussion regarding this question!

▶ *Question 3:* This is the key question of this section: finding the themes of the "Model Prayer," and incorporating them into the way we actually pray.

▶ *Optional Exercise:* This is a way of continuing the experience of group prayer by using written prayers. Some of the great themes for prayer are found in the "Model Prayer." See section III in the *Oxford Book of Prayer* for examples of the rich treasure of prayers on these themes.

Chapter Six: Worshiping God

6

Beginning

▶ Since the theme is worship, this exercise will help people to express their past and present experiences of church. Remember:
- Not everyone will have attended church as a child.
- Not all experiences of church are positive (since some churches are boring and irrelevant, especially to children). This means that some people have great psychological hurdles to get over in order for worship to become a rich experience for them.
- Few people still attend the church of their childhood. This is not necessarily bad. No denomination is perfect, and different worship styles fit different people at different phases in life. The important point is to be part of a worshiping community.

▶ *Question 1:* This discusses the experience of church (or the lack thereof).

▶ *Question 2:* The components of most church services are listed.

▶ *Question 3:* Experiences in worship shift from childhood to adulthood.

Understanding the Text

▶ *Question 1:* The Day of Pentecost was highly significant for the early church. It was the day when the Holy Spirit descended in power. (You will want to read all of Acts 2 for the full context.) This question is designed as an observation question that will make sure people have noticed what is in the passage. So don't spend a lot of time on this question.

▶ *Question 2:* At this point, you are only interested in the basic definition of these terms and events. This is not the time for a heated discussion about what it means to receive the Holy Spirit!

▶ *Question 3:* You should focus on these four aspects of church life.

▶ *Question 4:* You may not get to question 4. The discussion of question 3 may take all of your time. If you do get to question 4:
  • Have people read Acts 2:14–36 in their own Bibles (since it will take too long to read it aloud).
  • Emphasize that they are to scan it (not read it in depth). Otherwise, question 4 will take up far too much time.
  • They are to look for the main points, which are:
    • Peter begins by explaining to the crowd what they have just witnessed.
    • This is the pouring out of God's Spirit.
    • This was foretold by the prophet Joel (whom he quotes).
    • Peter then explains who Jesus is.
    • He was a man who did miracles (as they knew).
    • The miracles were a sign that God was working through Jesus.
    • However, they put him to death.
    • But God raised him from the dead,
    • as David foretold.
    • Peter explains the resurrection.
    • The point is that God raised Jesus from the dead.
    • The apostles are witnesses to this fact.
    • Jesus has been exalted to the right hand of God.
    • From there he has sent the Holy Spirit,
    • as they have just witnessed,
    • as David foretold.
    • The conclusion: Jesus is Lord and Messiah.

▶ If time is short, you may want to summarize the main points rather than have the group discuss Peter's sermon.

▶ The purpose of question 4 is to:
  • Understand better the meaning of the coming of the Holy Spirit.
  • Recall the facts of the gospel.
  • Catch some of the wonder these pious Jews must have felt as they were firsthand witnesses to the power of God and the fulfillment of prophecy.

▶ *Optional Exercise:* This is a role-play discussion in which you ask people to put themselves in the place of the pious Jews and to re-experience this amazing event. If you have an adventurous group, you might even want to do an actual role-play. Ask three group members to pretend they were there on the Day of Pentecost. Have them explain to a fourth person what happened, what they understood, how they felt, and what they did (they were among the 3,000 who were converted to Christ).

Applying the Text
  ▶ *Question 1:* Continue to explore the conversion of the 3,000. The experience of group members will parallel the experience of the 3,000, and will provide an easy way of talking about what happened to them.
  ▶ *Question 2:* Shift now to what each of the four aspects of church life looks like today.
    • Explore the teaching ministry of the church in its many forms: sermons, adult education, Sunday school, CCD, confirmation classes, small group Bible study, etc.

- Explore the various expressions of fellowship. What is community life together like? How is caring expressed? What relational networks exist? What events draw people in the church together?
- How is Communion celebrated, and what role does it play in the life of the church?
- Explore the prayer life of the church in all its forms: prayer in the worship service, prayer groups, teaching about prayer, types of prayer in the church, private prayer, prayer books, etc.

▶ *Question 3:* This is the heart of the discussion: an exploration of the role worship plays in our lives.

▶ *Questions 4 and 5:* The amount of time you have to explore these questions will vary. If you have ample time, read the two other passages mentioned in the *Comment* section and discuss the meaning of Communion and baptism. If you are short on time, you may want to make a few comments and encourage people to think about these matters during the week.

▶ *Optional Question:* This is an extension of question 3. It moves the discussion from the general (the role of worship in the life of believers) to the specific (the role of worship in each group member's life). You may want to combine this question with the discussion of question 3.

Other Materials

▶ The article on the church by John Stott is a concise and accurate statement of its role in the life of believers and is well worth a thorough reading. The *Reflection Questions* will enable each person to apply the ideas to his or her life.

Chapter Seven: Following God

7

Beginning

▶ The aim of this conversation (aside from the usual goal of allowing people to tell their stories and getting them in touch with each other) is to begin thinking about the process of pilgrimage. Although this focuses on one kind of pilgrimage (our vocational pilgrimage), it relates to the theme of spiritual pilgrimage (in that it is often through our vocations that we can serve God).

▶ *Question 1:* Most kids speculate on their future occupations (as a firefighter, doctor, farmer, etc.).

▶ *Question 2:* But over time, plans change. We discover our dream occupation is not nearly as attractive as we imagined; we see a host of other options we did not know about as a kid; we discover certain skills or interests that can be turned into a vocation.

▶ *Question 3:* However, we are not locked into a given vocation. Increasingly, adults are making (sometimes radical) switches in vocation. Is God calling you in new directions?

Understanding the Text

▶ *Question 1:* Even though this is basically an observation question, it will encourage good discussion (since faith is not an easy term to get a handle on). See the *Bible Study Notes* for help in understanding what faith is.

▶ *Question 2:* This set of questions will direct the group to notice the nature and meaning of Abraham's journey. His journey is the metaphor for the journey of faith.

▶ *Question 4:* Even though this focuses on paragraph four of the passage, it also serves as a summation question for the whole passage.

▶ *Question 5:* This question focuses on the final paragraph. Be sure to notice the dynamic and powerful way that Peterson has translated this paragraph—so that we are challenged and encouraged by it.

▶ *Optional Exercise:* Paraphrasing is a valuable way to see if you understand a passage. If you can't put the passage in your own words, you have not yet fully understood it. This exercise has an interesting twist to it. The group is asked to paraphrase a paraphrase (which is the nature of Peterson's translation).

Applying the Text

▶ *Question 1:* This question picks up from (and builds upon) question 1 in the previous section.

▶ *Question 2:* This question moves from the practical meaning of faith (question 1) to the practical meaning of pilgrimage. The aim of the discussion is to help the group to see how thinking about life in these terms causes us to live in a certain way.

▶ *Question 3:* This moves from the general discussion of pilgrimage (in question 2) to a more specific discussion of how Abraham's journey of faith is a model for our journeys of faith.

▶ *Question 4:* Now the discussion moves to the role of hope in our lives.

▶ *Question 5:* Finally, each group member is asked to think of his or her life as a pilgrimage.

▶ *Optional Exercise:* The focus in this exercise is on specific events that have shaped or defined the nature and direction of our pilgrimages. For example, a young woman may have received a call to the mission field during a church service (and this caused her to move in new directions educationally and vocationally). Noticing such defining events is important in constructing the specific shape of each person's pilgrimage.

Farewell Party: Since this is the final session in this book, set aside some time to bring a formal conclusion to the series. Some of the things you might consider doing include:

▶ *Share memories:* Ask group members to recall the best moments in the group (as well as the worst moments!). What did they especially appreciate about the group? What did they learn?

▶ *Pray together:* Commit the whole series to God. Ask God to take all that you have learned and use it in your lives. Let this be an extended time instead of a brief concluding prayer. You might want to bring some prayers to use (from the *Oxford Book of Prayer*), or you might want to give people time to write out prayers they will pray. You can also discuss as a group what to pray about. In any case, let this be a time of praise, thanksgiving, and commitment.

▶ *Plan the next series of small group sessions:* You may want to take a one and two week break before you begin again (or you may need to take a longer break if Christmas, summer, or some other special time is coming). You may decide to continue meeting weekly. In any case, plan on doing Book

Two of this series: *Learning to Love Ourselves.*
- Decide whether to keep group membership the same or to invite new members. Some group members may not be able to attend the new series. Bid them farewell. Think about how you can recruit new members. Or you may decide that one or two of your group will form a new group to go through *Learning to Love God* again with new people.
- Decide how the next group will be led.

▶ *Have a party:* Arrange for the kind of food and drink that will produce a good celebration. Enjoy each other. After all, a party is all about being with friends in a relaxed atmosphere—and you have made new friends during these seven weeks (and have deepened old friendships).

SMALL-GROUP MATERIALS FROM NAVPRESS

BIBLE STUDY SERIES

DESIGN FOR DISCIPLESHIP
GOD IN YOU
GOD'S DESIGN FOR THE FAMILY
INSTITUTE OF BIBLICAL
  COUNSELING Series

LEARNING TO LOVE Series
LIFECHANGE
LOVE ONE ANOTHER
STUDIES IN CHRISTIAN LIVING
THINKING THROUGH DISCIPLESHIP

TOPICAL BIBLE STUDIES

Becoming a Woman of Excellence
Becoming a Woman of Freedom
Becoming a Woman of Purpose
The Blessing Study Guide
Celebrating Life
Homemaking
Intimacy with God
Loving Your Husband

Loving Your Wife
A Mother's Legacy
Praying From God's Heart
Surviving Life in the Fast Lane
To Run and Not Grow Tired
To Walk and Not Grow Weary
What God Does When Men Pray
When the Squeeze Is On

BIBLE STUDIES WITH COMPANION BOOKS

Bold Love
Daughters of Eve
The Discipline of Grace
The Feminine Journey
Inside Out
The Masculine Journey
The Practice of Godliness
The Pursuit of Holiness

Secret Longings of the Heart
Spiritual Disciplines
Tame Your Fears
Transforming Grace
Trusting God
What Makes a Man?
The Wounded Heart
Your Work Matters to God

RESOURCES

Brothers!
How to Build a Small Groups Ministry
How to Lead Small Groups
Jesus Cares for Women
The Navigator Bible Studies
  Handbook

The Small Group Leaders
  Training Course
Topical Memory System
  (KJV/NIV and NASB/NKJV)
Topical Memory System:
  Life Issues

VIDEO PACKAGES

Bold Love
Hope Has Its Reasons
Inside Out
Living Proof

Parenting Adolescents
Unlocking Your Sixth Suitcase
Your Home, A Lighthouse